Missing the Point

The rise of High Modernity and the decline of everything else

John Elsom

To Ann & John
Many thanks for your help over the years (and, more important, friendships)
Happy Christmas ~
love
Sally + John

The Lutterworth Press

The Lutterworth Press
P.O. Box 60
Cambridge
CB1 2NT

www.lutterworth.com
publishing@lutterworth.com

ISBN 978 0 7188 3075 5

British Library Cataloguing in Publication Data
A catalogue record is available from the British Library

Copyright © John Elsom, 2007

First published in 2007

Contents

Preface   5

Acknowledgements   6

1. In the Negev Desert   7

2. Good Resolutions and a Dome   20

3. Two Thousand Five Hundred Years of Modernity   34

4. Man at the Mercy of Measurement Systems   47

5. The Trouble with Artists   60

6. The Irish Peace Process   74

7. The Perception Managers   89

8. The Declining Skills of Rhetoric   102

9. The Taming of the Beeb   114

10. The Shaping of Experience   127

11. Zeitgeist   139

12. Revelation   150

Index   162

Also by
John Elsom

Books

Theatre outside London
Erotic Theatre
Post-War British Theatre
The History of the National Theatre (with Nicholas Tomalin)
The Arts – Change and Choice
Post-War British Theatre Criticism
The Shaping of Experience
Cold War Theatre

Plays

Peacemaker
The Well-Intentioned Builder
One More Bull
How I Coped
Malone Dies
(Adapted from Samuel Beckett's novel for the comic actor, Max Wall)
The Man of the Future is Dead

Maui (a libretto for the opera by Barry Anderson)

Preface

This book has taken a long time to complete. I am writing this final touch, a preface, on the day that Tony Blair is stepping down as the British Prime Minister, but it began more than twelve years ago, when John Major was in 10 Downing Street and Bill Clinton at the White House. This is a long time in anybody's politics. Indeed, it was plotted in my mind even before then, at the end of the Cold War, as a long essay for the US magazine, *The World & I*, on why George Bush Sr.'s New World Order was not new, not global and, except as a way of helping us all to conform to the myths of modernity, not orderly. It was never published.

I was then the chair of a very small cultural NGO, the International Association of Theatre Critics, affiliated to UNESCO, and from this moderate podium, we had what could be described as a navel-high view of international politics, witnessing the gut reactions and the winds of change that blew statesmen in and out of office. We never mixed with them socially. It would have been unprofessional to do so. It was as if we were always in our places in the stalls, scribbling away and trying to make sense of the plots that were taking place on the stage above.

It was surprisingly easy to do so. Political life rarely imitates art, but it has an infinite capacity to absorb theatrical clichés. Who could fail to guess that Blair's six-week long ride into the sunset of his prime-ministerial career might end with a visit to the Pope and from Governor Schwarzenegger, in that order? Or, to take an earlier example, that the massacre of whole herds of cows, tens of thousands of them, in a foot-and-mouth epidemic, would reach a final photo-call with a calf, doe-eyed, a family pet, saved from the slaughter by soft-hearted and publicity-conscious government agents?

Improvisation? Not much of it. Most political leaders have the unfortunate habit of trying to live up to their original conclusions – or promises – so that even the events of 9/11 were employed to implement the Neo-Cons' agenda by invading Iraq and Afghanistan. Rather like inferior jazz musicians, who use the apparent freedom of jazz to repeat old riffs, so politicians, when confronted by the unexpected, try to regain control of events by reacting as predictably as possible.

This may not be their fault. In a democracy, they have to behave in a conventional way to retain the support of their electors. All successful politicians reflect the climate of opinion, the *zeitgeist*, that brought them to power. They are the expressions of culture – and sometimes even its victims – which is why it is helpful to have theatre critics, sitting in the stalls to comment upon how well or ill they perform. The supreme skill that distinguishes the mature critic from the rest of mankind, is to have seen it all before – to know why stories are constructed in this way, why characters conform to type and why we are expected to think as we do. This book might be described as a critical review of the drama of our times, but this particular play can never be repeated. It simply unfolds.

This is where the analogy with the theatre breaks down, for there are no intervals in international politics, no comfort breaks to relieve yourself, although the happenings on stage may prompt you to do so very publicly, no ice-creams or gin-and-tonics, and you can only leave the theatre once, never to return. All one can hope to do is to offer a description, an analysis and a temporary record – as I do now.

Acknowledgements

This book has taken its toll on those closest to me. They read and re-read the drafts; and commented upon them with love and patience. They were my best critics, my unseen editors and my sources of inspiration. Without them, this book could not have been written. But there were others less close, who commented on the drafts from more detached points of view, responding in a friendly way to a request from me. I am grateful to my colleagues in the IATC, my students and former students, and those from the Arab world, whom I met through the Cairo International Festival of Experimental Theatre. I must particularly thank Martin Banham, Nicole Boireau, John Calder, Sir David Fell, Angela Godfrey-Goldstein, Anthony Field CBE, Charles Hill QC, Emma Hutson, Welton Jones, David Li Yan, Jenny McCartney, Cal McCrystal, John McLoughlin, Richard Mead, Michael Meadowcroft, Paul Medlicott, Anna Miran, Catalina Panaitescu, John Pick, Paul Reynolds, Ricard Salvat, Irving Wardle and Noel Witts. A special debt of gratitude must go to my dedicated agent, Judith Elliott. When other literary agents had given up the task of selling this book in its earlier drafts, she found the right publisher, Adrian Brink, and the right publishing house, Lutterworth.

Chapter One
In the Negev Desert

In 1963, the Israeli government made a generous gesture towards the Bedouin tribes who lived in the Negev desert, the one group of neighbouring Arabs not hostile to the State of Israel. It gave them land. It lent them money, so that they could build houses. Since the shortage of water was a continual problem, it installed pipelines across the desert, so that they could enjoy the benefits of civilization, like any other Israeli citizen. But the Bedouins were nomads. For centuries, they had travelled across this arid region in family groups, herding their flocks of goats and camels. They did not own or even value land. The wealth of aristocratic Bedouins came from the family guardianship of water wells, where there might be grazing and trading. The all-too-convenient pipelines threatened to impoverish them and to destroy their way of life.

It may seem odd to begin a book about cultural politics in the Negev desert, where there are no opera houses or theatres. In Britain, we are often given the impression that culture and the arts are so closely related that they amount to the same thing. The title of New Labour's Department of Culture, Media and Sport suggests as much, where *culture* refers to the government office mainly devoted to the arts, but this is like confusing the swimmer with the sea. It is not in dispute that artists live and work within a culture. That they can influence and even change the direction of a culture is also not in doubt. The extent of that influence and whether a culture can flourish without them are much more controversial questions.

"Culture" derives from a Latin word for "a cultivated strip of land" or "the act of cultivation". By extension, it came to mean a group of people, a society, where human beings could live and work together because they shared certain beliefs, a general outlook. Many of these assumptions, such as loyalty and human rights, could not be exactly proved. They could not be tested and confirmed by direct experience. The ancient Greeks used a special term for an unprovable assumption, *mūthos*, from which the modern word, myth, is derived. Its exact opposite was *logos*, which meant a word or a symbol, whose meaning could be tested by experience or reason acting upon experience. All languages, according to the ancient Greeks, contained provable and unprovable elements, even the language of mathematics, although it may have been a mistake to imply that these aspects could be kept apart.

But the word, "myth", has come to mean a story that was false or untrue, not just unprovable. That is even more misleading. Societies require myths. They cannot function without them. But how can the would-be members of a society be persuaded to share ideas that cannot be proved or tested? The answer often lay with the artists, the acknowledged mythmakers, whose skills at music, storytelling and painting fired the imagination and brought to the mind's eye the plausible un-realities.

Once accepted, myths can become so deeply embedded in the mental habits of a society that, like the programming of a computer, they are only noticed when they go wrong. This is why they are sometimes best seen from a distance, such as the Negev desert. When one group of people, which believes that land is property but that water should be free, comes into contact with another, which is equally convinced that water is property but that land should be free, even a gesture of good will can go badly astray. In the Negev desert, it turned peaceful neighbours into enemies and united Bedouin families against the State of Israel as they had rarely been united before.

Much rested upon these myths. The Israeli government was not simply being generous. It was asserting its territorial rights. It wanted to secure its borders. It did not want to stop and search the nomadic families to see if there might be terrorists among them. But it may also have honestly believed that it was offering the Bedouins a better way of life – with roads, hospitals and welfare systems – all of which rested upon their sharing the basic Western assumption of land ownership.

The Bedouins thought differently. In their view, the government was giving them something that they did not want, land, in exchange for the control over something that they prized highly, water. Not only were their lifestyles and freedom to roam being challenged, but their religious beliefs, their customs and etiquette, and their ways of settling disputes as well. To forbid a stranger from drinking at one of their wells was a hostile act, almost a declaration of war, but to drink without permission was an offence against the laws of hospitality, no better than theft. Where was all that water coming from anyway? Were lawless strangers, who did not apprehend the secrets of the desert, disturbing the balance of nature? The Bedouins' understanding of the world, in short, their culture, was at stake.

What cannot be proved cannot be disproved. Myths may not be true or false, but some are more plausible than others, more useful or necessary to the running of daily life. To prevent the solid myths on which a stable society depends from sinking into the mire of relativity, all politicians, even in liberal democracies, seek to regulate the myths in circulation. This is the familiar side to cultural politics, the routine practice of handing out broadcasting franchises and grants to the arts (or withholding them), for the enigmatic sentence on the foundation stone of every bureaucratic structure erected to implement a cultural policy is simply this: who licenses the mythmakers?

But, on another level, all politics is cultural politics, inevitably so. All political parties have their narratives of history. All politicians have their favourite myths but, since these may be as much at odds as those of the Israelis and the Bedouins, all societies develop ways of avoiding conflict and of choosing the most appropriate myths in fair or not-so-fair contests. Liberal democracy is just one of the methods; for the peaceful construction and de-construction of alternative myths goes on all the time, everywhere, in the market place, the boardroom and the sports field; and through such processes of adjustment, civilizations quietly evolve.

Some myths, however, are hostile to others and unwilling to tolerate rivals. Sometimes events take control and there is too little time or living space for adjustment. Sometimes we are confronted by starkly opposing myths, which cry out for us to support them against all the others. Sometimes it is necessary to have the courage of our convictions and defend what seem to be the better myths against the worse ones, even though none can be proved. Sometimes we may do so with our lives. In those circumstances, it is often hard to remember the humbling first law of cultural politics, the nitty-gritty. Since none of us have access to absolute truth, what limited version of whose partial truth will prevail?

In 1981, some eighteen years after this example occurred of how to annoy the neighbours by being nice to them, I had the opportunity to meet a Bedouin chief in his new home in the Negev desert. His tent was pitched in an empty space, which looked like a parking lot in the middle of a housing estate. One camel chewed at its tether outside. Inside, the tent was comfortably spread with carpets and cushions. An Israeli guide and interpreter came with me, although our host spoke English. We were served with mint tea from a silver tea service. In some respects, it felt like an old-fashioned English tea party, polite but barbed.

My guide wanted to show me how well the Bedouins were being treated, in spite of their hostility to the state. They had been allowed to keep their arts and crafts, but given the benefits of civilization as well, such as running water, nearby. But our host had evidently decided that I was part of his problem. He did not want to be presented to the outside world as an object of Israeli benevolence. My guide asked him how his grandchildren were doing at school, hinting that in the desert they might not have been educated at all. "I rarely see them," he replied and added that he went to university himself, where he had studied Islamic law. He would not be patronised as an illiterate, just because he was living in reduced circumstances, through no fault of his own.

In the eyes of the outside world, the State of Israel had changed as well. In 1963, it had been a threatened enclave, where Jewish refugees had fled from the holocaust and pure socialism was practised in its *kibbutzim*. After its six-day war with Egypt in 1967, when it seized the Sinai peninsular and captured the towns of Bethlehem and Hebron from Jordan, it was the most powerful force in the region, Israel the Schnitzel, "the more you beat it, the more it expands". By 1981, it had built new settlements on the occupied West Bank of the Jordan, and threatened to invade southern Lebanon, although it had not yet done so. To prevent the outside world from presuming that its successes in war had turned it into a bully, the Friends of Israel, registered as a British charity, invited some Western journalists to see for themselves how well the peaceful Arabs were being treated, which was how I came to be sitting in a tent in the Negev desert.

I had an axe to grind as well. I was collecting examples of heritage protection. I was a free lance writer whose main employer was the BBC, but I had taken on two jobs as the vice-chair (and then the chair) of the British Liberal Party's Arts and Broadcasting Committee and as a committee member (and later its president) of a cultural NGO, affiliated to UNESCO, the International Association of Theatre Critics, "making the world a better place for theatre critics". These were unpaid and time-consuming posts, and shamefully ineffectual, with high ambitions. We were facing such questions as the future of broadcasting, the threats to the live arts and the likely collapse of the Soviet empire, but "heritage" was high on our agenda.

Heritage was the vogue word. In the 1970s, UNESCO started to compile a list of world heritage sites, beginning with the Polish city of Krakow and the cathedral at Chartres in France. The Barbican Centre in London – a Modernist sprawl of tower blocks, offices and performance spaces

– had a Heritage Walkway, where fragments of the medieval city walls were incongruously preserved and visible. The first ministry of culture in Britain, under a Conservative government, was called the Department for National Heritage. Heritage meant different things to different people. For some, it was akin to ancestor worship, for others it was more of a matter of building museums. Heritage was supposed to have something to do with national identity. It was widely feared that many identities would be lost beneath layers of Anglo-American imperialism.

My task was to find a definition of 'heritage', which was appropriate for the British Liberal Party. I sought clear water between the patriotism on the right and the political correctness on the left. Some Liberals showed signs of what might be called the Laurens-van-der-Postian tendency. They firmly believed that those who lived in the desert had a better understanding of the ways of God than those who built roads across it. What should be retained were not the ethnic artefacts that could be found in any market place, but the spiritual insights that these cultures contained. Traces of them were embedded in the indigenous languages. The Bedouin had as many words for sand as the Inuit had for snow, displaying an understanding of their territory that an ecologist would envy.

To meet a Bedouin chief in the Negev desert was an opportunity to confirm a liberal myth, but my first impression was that he was a hunting trophy on the walls of progress, but alive, not stuffed, and fully capable of shooting back. He was surrounded by objects that had once reminded his visitors of his wealth and authority, but now, shorn of their power to persuade, seemed little more than trinkets. Among the many millions of those who are, or think that they are, the victims of Western cultural imperialism, he was not an unfortunate man. His primary language, Arabic, was not under threat, nor his Islamic faith. But he was very bitter. He resented the life that he was forced to live and indicated as much in dry, ironic remarks.

He could find his way around the town, but this was not the same as living in the desert where he could survive without relying upon the local supermarket. Some relatives lived nearby. He sometimes stayed with them, but the ties of his extended family were broken. Others had left the region to seek more remote places. Those who lived in the town were mainly *fellaheen*, Egyptian Arabs whom aristocratic Bedouin had once treated like a servant class. He had been forced to place his own mother in a home, something that could never have happened in the old days. Arab families always looked after their elderly relatives. Who would look after him in his old age?

My Israeli guide started to look uneasy. He described the social services that were, or shortly would be, looking after him, but gave up the attempt. "What about your wife?" he asked, "Your own wife?" and added for my benefit, "Which one was she, the third or fourth? Didn't she go to hospital? Wasn't she cured?" "She was cut open," the chief replied, as if his property had been damaged, "She healed."

"She went to the best hospital in Beer-Sheba," the guide stated, "It is world-famous! And her treatment was absolutely free." He turned to me for support. But the chief spread his hands, indicating the range of his possessions, as if to say, "You take my liberty, my family possessions and my pride, and you tell me that this is free?" The guide shook his head sadly, such ingratitude! But added, as if to clinch his case, "Well, you have a vote like anyone else..."

My host smiled like a predatory barrister. He carefully explained how much he thought that his vote was worth, which was very little. There were Arab deputies in the Knesset, the Israeli parliament. They were worth very little as well. Democracy promoted the Western belief in human equality, much to its credit perhaps, but for many like him, it lacked moral values and common sense. The ballot box made no distinction between the young and the old, the good and the bad, the ignorant and the educated. It turned upside down the time-honoured custom whereby a man earned the respect of others by behaving well and acting wisely, and was thus entitled to take decisions. In other words, he concluded, democracy was a confidence trick that duped the gullible into thinking that they had political influence, whereas they had none at all – or perhaps too much for their own good.

He looked at me as if challenging me to disagree, but I buried my head in my notebook and said nothing. I sensed the approach of an unanswerable question. Which of them was right? Each believed that he was right. Each was convinced that a fair-minded observer would recognise that truth was on his side. Each was ready to relate the history of his race to prove that land ownership was better than water ownership, or vice versa, and that the laws of nature, as well as heritage, were on his side. Their perceptions of reality, structured by their myths, were at odds. Since neither could be proved, the gulf was unbridgeable. One was right and the other was wrong. Which?

This was the kind of question that I, equally structured, was trained to avoid. As a contributor to the BBC, where the obligation to be impartial was written into its Royal Charter, I usually tried to present both sides of the story to let the listener decide. As a reporter, I was taught that facts (and only facts) were sacred. In the UK, we were facing a turbulent year – with race riots in Brixton and Toxteth, riots in Belfast after the deaths of two IRA hunger strikers, confrontations with the trade unions and high unemployment – in which the sphinx-like riddle, *which is right*, cried out from every rooftop. In the midst of this turmoil, we started to feel the cooling influence of post-modernity. All sides – and none of them – were right. That was the answer.

Post-modernism threw a very large bucket of cold water over the ideals and principles for which our parents and grandparents had fought. Not for the first time in its history, Platonism with its myths of absolutes and essences was out of fashion. A person might be right from his or her point of view, but had no business to impose that point of view upon others. When translated into economic terms, this meant sacrificing the tempting prizes of the command economy for the uncertainties of the market. To govern meant primarily the management of a country, whose state-run institutions were assets or liabilities to be bought and sold in the interests of the electorate at large, its share- or stake- holders. The sacred cows of the welfare state became its sacrificial lambs. When they were not being slaughtered, they were being threatened with a big knife and told to behave properly. Led by Mrs Thatcher's government, we were taking a long, sceptical look at the unprovable assumptions that had contributed to the building of post-war Britain and were prepared to throw them all away – ruthlessly, if necessary.

The belief that such institutions as the BBC should educate and enlighten, as well as entertain, came under attack from left and right. The values of Auntie Beeb, it was said, reflected the views of a small group, the Oxbridge elite, who ignored the changing demographic patterns in the UK. The same might be said of the Arts Council. The answer on the right was to transform them into more business-like enterprises, in which the management conducted its market research, respected the wishes of its customers and supplied the cultural goods that they really wanted.

Those on the left who had been warned that money was the root of all evils deplored this commercial approach. One of their aims was to create an open society, rather like an open marriage, not committed to any one party or point of view, where all races and ethnic groups would feel at home. Old Britain, the Britain of the British Empire, stuffy class-bound, white Britain, with its queues and English Gothic, stood in its way. Cultures, however, may not always be so compatible. They may undermine each other. If so, there may be troubles ahead.

The eccentricities of supposedly old-fashioned cultures, like the British, conceal what may be called mechanisms for avoiding trouble, such as politeness, formal debates and competitive sports. Cultures like these are packed to the brim with ways of getting out of serious confrontations without losing face.

Such rituals to preserve the peace are most appreciated when, as in the Negev desert, they are in short supply. As a guest of the Friends of Israel and a Bedouin chief, I did not have to decide which was *ultimately* right and I could have let myself off the hook by being ironic about the whole non-event, but the unspoken questions would still twist in the mind. Did I support Israel in this matter – or the Bedouin Arabs – and to what extent? Or could I avoid them forever by sitting on the fence of post-modernity?

Liberals in those days passionately believed in the open society. It was one of the few matters on which we all agreed. We were of the opinion that a dominant culture should not dictate to a minority culture, but if, as in Northern Ireland, the two cultures seemed irreconcilable, or if, as in the Negev desert, the politics of conquest reduced the Bedouin culture to a tea party in a parking lot, we post-modern Liberals tended to be evasive. Frankly, it was one of our faults. Our opponents were scathing. Liberals, they said, could never make up their minds about anything. That was unfair. We had made up our minds that cultural diversity was a good thing and that all institutions should be multi-cultural, and we firmly believed that, if they were, many of the conflicts that arose when one culture threatens another would simply disappear.

Unfortunately, a policy of cultural diversity always seemed to demand a great deal of social engineering. The prime example was Northern Ireland, with its official policy of "parity of esteem" between two "equally valid" cultural traditions. Despite post-modernity, the freethinking radicals on the left were never slow to interfere. They called it positive discrimination. It involved the physical and metaphorical de-construction of national institutions, such as the BBC, to get rid of its cultural biases, and the construction of new institutions, which were called by the same names, dedicated to the idea that the state should be open and inclusive.

But some devices for avoiding trouble, once taken apart, might not be so easy to put together again. The old BBC was full of them. The belief in an open society came to mean that the answer to the question, 'which is right?', should be avoided for as long as possible. A government that revealed its cultural preferences no longer seemed impartial, but, sadly, the one that did not simply stagnated. Sooner or later, minds had to be made up.

In the Negev desert, home of spiritual revelations, I experienced a change of heart that stopped just short of a Damascene conversion. There was no such thing as an open society. It was a contraction in terms. No government could treat all cultures equally, as if it were above the battle itself. This was philosophically unsound – and might lead towards totalitarianism – for it assumed that a Modernist state could embrace every shade of belief known to man, which was absurd. It was the most arrogant myth of them all.

The Negev tea party taught me another lesson. The more I was impartially polite, the more agitated my guide and my host became. If I agreed with my guide that the hospital in Beersheba was very fine, he glared at me as if to say, "What's wrong with it?" If I listened to my host's account of the old days, took notes and asked if he had ever thought of writing a book, his response was to spit in the sand. They did not want soothing remarks. To the ardently committed, "objectivity" or, in their view, "moral equivalence" was the worst betrayal. The stand off was three-way.

And so the mint tea ran cold, and we averted our eyes from each other, and with the coolest of cool handshakes, we went our separate ways. At my hotel, I felt very uneasy. Such cultural rifts could spread anywhere. They could fragment the very ground under our feet. My Israeli guide could put on his military uniform and take up his gun, and my Bedouin host could slip away into the sand hills, and they might blow each other up, and anyone like me who came in their way. And this, broadly speaking, was what happened. I never saw my Bedouin host again, but I feel his eyes upon me whenever I switch on a television set and wonder about what he might make of our Anglo-American faction, our news and entertainment mixture. He would be in a better position than I am to guess whether our efforts to spread freedom and democracy in the Middle East stand any chance of success.

After the Cold War, the West was left with a combination of advantages that had few, if any, parallels in modern history. The United States was the last remaining global superpower, militarily and economically. It had friendly, but not uncritical, relations with other rich countries, which in the eyes of the rest of the world were lumped together collectively as "the West". Nor was this dominance solely based upon materialism and greed. Western liberal democracies stood firm against two would-be world dictatorships, and outlasted them. They provided their citizens with higher living standards, better social services – and, against all expectations, more fairness and social cohesion.

For a short period of time, the West could claim a moral leadership to back up its other advantages, but this drift towards goodwill went into reverse after an extraordinary series of miscalculations. The bombing of Belgrade by NATO forces during the campaign in Kosovo sent out signals to the countries of the former Soviet Union that they might become targets in the future. As a result, Russia and Ukraine, two nuclear powers, signed a pact for their self-protection, a step backwards into the Cold War. The invasion of Afghanistan by US-led forces to root out Al-Qaeda and destroy the Taliban left the country with an imposed democratic government, whose authority ranged little beyond Kabul. The pre-emptive strike against Iraq by the "coalition of the willing" got rid of its dictator, Saddam Hossein, but divided NATO, weakened the UN's Security Council and damaged the reputation for truthfulness of the US and British governments.

It is possible that these adventures may yet turn out well and the efforts to impose democratic-looking governments, backed by the Allied forces, may survive and flourish, but the myths of liberal democracy that the allies were supposed to be promoting were confounded by the facts of their behaviour. These included the humiliation of detainees, the gunning down of unarmed civilians and the Guantanamo Bay detention centre, whose very existence flouted the Geneva Convention. The list of blunders was a long one and they gave the impression that the English-speaking West, when left without rivals, behaved no better than any other bully in the playground.

The US and British governments claimed was that their response was justified by the nature of the war against terror, which, unlike normal wars, had no rules of engagement. The events of 9/11 in New York, the train bombing in Madrid, the carnage at a Bali resort and the suicide bombings in London in 2005 were massacres, in which the terrorists made no distinction between civilians and the armed forces. It was thought reasonable that they should not be treated like other prisoners of war, but in a separate category. Both governments adopted such practices as detention without trial and secret interrogations, sometimes in other countries, which denied their suspects independent legal advice and broke at least two principles – or myths – of a free society.

The restraints upon the executive, which were meant to protect personal freedom, were relaxed in the measures against terrorism or in the name of better management. Soon the climate of opinion began to change, the *zeitgeist*, in which long-standing principles were routinely sacrificed to meet what appeared to be the needs of the moment. Constitutional lawyers were outraged and their sense of alarm was shared by large numbers of people. Nearly two million marched in London to protest against the war in Iraq, but, despite this, the ruling parties in both countries won substantial election victories. Those who wanted to believe in the soundness of the electoral systems were shocked by the statistical quirks. George W. Bush was elected to his first term as US president on a minority of the popular vote, after a wrangle over disputed 'chads' in the state of Florida. Tony Blair's Labour Party in Britain was even more fortunate. In 2005, it won a working *majority* after receiving 35.2% of the vote, the lowest total for any governing party in Europe, even less than Hitler's National Socialists gained when they became the largest *minority* party in the Reichstag in 1934. There was much public scepticism about the way in which political parties had come to sell their policies like any other product on the market – by spinning, perception management and 'astro-turfing',[1] which often crossed the border into mass deception.

In the eyes of a hostile observer, such as my Bedouin host in an Israeli parking lot, such examples must confirm the view that a liberal democracy could be as fragile and easily manipulated as the feudal regimes, religious oligarchies and proletarian dictatorships that the West was seeking to replace around the world. But in spreading its message, the West was helped by the astonishing developments in communications, driven by Western technology and media companies. From one point of view, this globalisation of the small-screen might seem to be a good thing, opening up isolated countries to the forces of Modernity, but it was a one-sided freedom, distorted by wealth and patterns of ownership.

Non-Western countries found it hard to escape, if they wanted to do so, from this kind of cultural imperialism. It could be very intrusive. It upset faiths and customs alike. The Indian government tried, and failed, to ban satellite dishes. In all Islamic countries, it aroused hostility to the West, even among the young, who might imitate its fashions, but still felt generally left out of the party. There were dissenters in the West as well. In their eyes too, the Free World itself had acquired the false glow of a sprayed-on bronze tan. Its 'grand narratives' – free speech, emancipation and the market (or social market) economy – were blended and diluted within a mixture that included fast cars, short skirts and fat-saturated hamburgers.

One Asian critic deplored "the vast movement towards the homogen-isation of culture, flowing from the West".[2] The very word, Modernity, meant westernisation. Even academic courses in Post-Colonial Studies had a Western ring. What post-colonialism? How can you talk about post-colonialism, when every skyline is dominated by Western-style skyscrapers, with Western-style electronic billboards, starring Western or Asian-Western companies, and financed by banks inspired by Western models, even if they did not, right now, have their headquarters in London or New York? How can you talk about post-colonialism, where every corner-shop college teaches its own version of US Business Management Studies? Surely even at the height of the British *raj*, Western interests did not so intrude and dominate the lives of the ordinary non-Western families.

In the West, we sometimes like to think that we live in a post-modern world (and some of us may), which tolerates every point of view and does not privilege any particular version of reality above another; but Blair's one-time champion, Anthony Giddens, was surely nearer the mark, when he asserted that we really live in an age of 'High Modernity',[3] where the myths of Modernity are so taken for granted that we no longer question them. And this perhaps was where our recent troubles started. It is tempting to believe that they were caused by wicked or naive men, but it may be more disconcerting, and yet more plausible, to suppose that they began with sincere and intelligent men, "better than average", motivated by myths that may not be exactly wrong, but were limited and at odds.

Myths are the tools of perception and we need a variety of them to form our impressions of the outside world, but we can become obsessed by our myths, and seek to impose them on every situation, often inappropriately, which is one reason why this book is called "Missing the Point". The true value of a myth, as the ancient Greeks explained, was not that it was unprovable, but that it was *revelatory*. It helped us to see reality more clearly. Those myths that turned their backs upon reality, and displayed merely their own inventiveness, missed the point at a far deeper level, which is a charge that can easily be laid against both High Modernity and Islamic Fundamentalism, together with other world religions.

But what has all this to do with cultural politics? My brief answer would be: "A great deal, in fact, almost everything!"

Notes

1. Astro-turfing was the term used when a political party tried to simulate a grass-roots movement in its favour by sending out similarly worded letters to local newspapers under false names or the names of party members, whose allegiances were concealed.
2. Dr. Sal Murgiyanto from Jakarta, Indonesia, speaking at an IATC Conference in Hong Kong, October, 2006.
3. See Giddens, *The Consequences of Modernity* (Polity Press, 1990), p.163. "We are currently living in an age of high modernity."

Chapter Two
Good Resolutions and a Dome

The coming of Second Millennium was celebrated throughout the world as the right time to make good resolutions. Its epicentre was the Greenwich Observatory in south London, a World Heritage site, three hundred years old, where East meets West at 0 degrees longitude and the Prime Meridian is engraved upon its paving stones. In the months before the start of the year 2000, tourists could go along to a Visitors Centre nearby, overlooking a building site, where the Millennium Dome was slowly being erected.

The Dome was Britain's most eye-catching contribution to the feast. Inside the Visitors Centre, there was a screen that boldly claimed: "Domes are the architecture of reverence and awe and Greenwich's Dome is the biggest of them all." Before the First Millennium, many feared that the world would end, but "now in a more confident age, we can look forward to a future which we believe we can, and must, control."

The country was basking in the glow of optimism that followed New Labour's landslide victory in 1997, when to raise a sceptical eyebrow was interpreted as a sign of dissent. But I was brought up in an older Britain that prided itself on understatement. We would not talk about controlling the future, however much we might hope to do so, because we had been warned about *hubris*, the wanton pride that attracted the wrath of Nemesis, goddess of vengeance. This diffidence might be a sham, and annoy those who thought that it was just another sign of conceit, but it was a habit of mind, which drew its strength from Anglicanism, eighteenth-century politeness and a classical education.

The Visitors Centre gave little indication as to what the Dome was for. We looked at computer screens, where its architectural drawings went around in elliptical circles, but the contents were being kept ostentatiously secret. The Dome, according to its historian, Adam Nicholson,[1] was "an act of the engineer's imagination, a fusion of the aesthetic, the functional and the daring needed to make the biggest roof in the world" – but a roof over what? To boast about controlling the future without knowing what was going to happen in the next few months seemed to me a rather reckless way to confront the midnight hour.

My fear was that the Dome would turn out to be another monument to Modernity, like an extremely large hypermarket or a theme park version of those big, mad books that were being published in the West, mostly in the US, since the end of the Cold War. They were big in the sense that they contained a lot of pages, big in their scale in that their perspective was global, big in that they were bloated with statistics, and gargantuan in their ambitions. They all described the New World Order, how it should be achieved and the obstacles in its way. All the thinkers and think tanks in the Free World seemed to be plotting how to make the best of the next thousand years, and publishing them in books, whose very size seemed to guarantee their seriousness.

Although these books were important and influential, few people seemed to have read them, and some were very hard to read. We knew about them from press releases, reviews and from hearing others talk about them. This was the first sign of madness. If we did read them, they often seemed well informed but curiously out-of-touch, long on fact but short on experience. We were told that as a result of globalisation, India was on the verge of an economic lift-off, but you did not have to travel far in the sub-continent to discover how undeveloped in a Western sense the country was. How many call centres had to be outsourced from Birmingham to Bangalore to pave the roads in Madurai?

Much of the research seemed to come from surfing the web. It was generally agreed that the US was the last remaining superpower and had a duty to lead the world towards a brighter future, but among the measurement systems that described its strength, there ran a vein of caution and even of paranoia. Its economy relied too much upon oil imported from unstable regimes in the Middle East. Its cities were vulnerable to terrorist attack. Malign forces were corrupting its youth with sex, violence and drugs. These big mad books were factual to a fault, but wedded to their beliefs with a fidelity rare in real marriages. You did not have to read far into their introductions to guess whether the authors came from the Noam-Chomsky-Left, the Neo-Cons or the soft-Clinton-Centre. They wore their myths on their sleeves, like hearts, but collectively they looked similar, dancing with the globe, like Charles Chaplin in *The Great Dictator*, which was why God, if he had been a good doctor, would have certified them instantly.

The battle of big mad books may be said to have began in 1989, the summer that saw the riots in Tienanmen Square and the collapse of the

Berlin Wall. The US political scientist, Francis Fukuyama, published an essay in *The National Interest*, "The End of History",[2] in which he argued: "we may be witnessing the end of history as such... the end point of mankind's ideological development and the universalization of Western liberal democracy." He expanded this theory into a best-selling book, but Samuel P. Huntington was among those who thought that Fukuyama was far too optimistic and wrote *The Clash of Civilizations*, another bestseller, to offer an alternative view.

Huntington feared that the political power of the West was in decline[3] and offered "a new paradigm"[4] for US foreign policy, in which he proposed that the world was sub-divided into nine major civilizations. The wars to take seriously were those on the "fault-line" where one civilization, such as Islam, came into conflict with another, as in the Middle East. The question arose as to whether the US and its allies should intervene to protect democracy, or to extend its range and influence, for "culture", in Huntington's estimation, "almost always follows power",[5] rarely the other way round.

Both books received endorsements at the highest level,[6] but as theoretical studies as to how the world might change for the better, they seemed to depend much upon guesswork. The Soviet Union may have collapsed, but this did not mean that the hour of democracy had come and it was odd to think of the continent of Africa as having just one civilization when it was a patchwork of so many. But in a free society, these broad-brush predictions were challenged by other writers of big mad books and quoted by the global management consultancies that provided a service for their clients by forecasting the shape of things to come. And so they entered the Western food chain of big, mad ideas.

The aims were almost always idealistic, even when the proposed methods might seem to lend themselves to abuse. Paul Wolfowitz, who became Bush's Deputy Secretary of Defence in 2001, was a theorist who helped to devise post-Cold War strategy. In 1989, his position was similar to that of Truman's adviser, George Kennan, after World War II. Both had been diplomats. Both were long-term foreign policy advisers, who served in the State Department, though there the similarities end. Kennan was an advocate of containment at a time when the Soviet Union was threatening the continent of Europe, but Wolfowitz argued for constructive intervention. With the danger of a Third World War receding, he believed that the US should take a lead in ridding the world of corrupt dictatorships. The Free World should intervene to save people from oppression and to protect us all from the threat of would-be Hitlers, even if the UN's Security Council was reluctant to do so.

Philip Bobbitt, an adviser to President Clinton, claimed that we were at a turning point in history, an ominous phrase, when the 'nation-state', as defined by territory, gave way to the 'market state', created by trading zones and common codes of behaviour. The European Union was one example. "The market state," he wrote, "promises a virtuous circle to those states that copy its form and obey its strictures."[7] But Bobbitt alarmed another commentator, Robert Harvey, who said that he had "consigned the painstakingly built structure of international law to the scrap heap".[8] The United Nations recognised "nation states", not "virtuous circles". Who would sit where in what debating chamber?

Harvey was British. He was a supporter of the United States and of liberal democracy in general, but as a former MP, he had not forgotten the tortuous processes through which decisions in a democracy are reached – and perhaps the wrong decisions. He described democracy as "Government by Talking Shop", which was hardly a rallying cry for the rest of the world. His own big book, *The Return of the Strong: The Drift to Global Disorder*,[9], was not about how the New World Order could be established, but about how the next world war could be avoided. He warned discreetly and handed out no visions. He was by temperament and party affiliations a Conservative.

New Labour on the other hand wanted to shed the image of a Britain that called for caution in challenging times. According to *The Blair Revolution*, by Peter Mandelson and Roger Liddle, published in 1997,[10] the British felt "increasingly insecure" in a time of "rapid economic and technological change".[11] The country was in decline and "badly equipped to meet the challenge of change". The scepticism of someone like Harvey was brushed aside as another sign of weakness. The answer was to tackle the "vested interests and class barriers" that held Britain back and release the "dynamism and entrepreneurial energy" of its people. "The fundamental question is whether we can compete successfully in the new global market-place and still live in a decent society."

This problem was confronted by another Blair supporter, Anthony Giddens, the social scientist who wrote *The Third Way* and introduced the words, "disembedding" and "structuration" into the English language. According to Giddens, we lived in a world not of post-modernity but High Modernity, in which science and the new technologies inevitably altered the way in which we lived. Mankind had to adjust to the discoveries of science, not the other way round, but this entailed changing our habits and uprooting ourselves from our former life-styles, or "disembedding".

Social structures would have to change too and the processes which brought them into being, hence "structuration".

In his vivid phrase, we had to learn how to ride "the Juggernaut of Modernity".[12] The New Millennium Experience, which was billed to occupy the Dome, "one amazing day", was intended to demonstrate to the people the opportunities and pitfalls of the age; the wonder and mystery of the technology; and what New Labour precisely meant by "a decent society". It was more than a political marketing ploy. It was to be an educational playground, where we could all learn how to ride the Juggernaut of Modernity without falling off. From this point of view, which was as much of a squint as a vista, the Dome would be inspirational, leading us towards a future that we "can, and must, control".

Large myths are often revealed by small details.

I am writing this chapter on a laptop in a hotel bedroom in Zagreb, the capital city of an independent nation, Croatia, which was recently part of a federation of states, old Yugoslavia, and now, in the first flush of its new patriotism, has applied to join another would-be federation, the European Union (EU). My computer was supplied with a word-processing package, Microsoft Word, developed in the United States. It has many useful programmes, among them a spelling and grammar check, which underlines the misspelt words in red and the grammatical errors in green.

It is not arrogant. It is polite. It invites me to change the spelling, but I am allowed to ignore its proposals. It knows that I am English and not American. In an earlier version of the spell-check, words with an English variant, such as theatre, were Americanized as *theater*, but now the English (UK) version anglicises the US spellings, which shows that a global corporation can be sensitive to the demands of the regional market. It is reliable to the extent that I can get into the habit of accepting its recommendations, but if I do, and look back upon what we have both written together, I find that what I had meant to say has been subtly altered. In particular, the grammar check dislikes the passive mood.

If I write, "We were converted to Christianity by a door-to-door salesman", it will underline the sentence in green and propose an alternative: "A door-to-door salesman converted us to Christianity". In one way, this is an improvement. It is a simpler, pithier sentence. But the accumulation of such sentences, in which the doer takes pride-of-place from the person to whom things are done, leaves a distinctly American impression. It is bright, positive and relentlessly can-do. It subtly evokes the history of the United States. The transformation of a half-continent by waves of immigrants from Europe and Africa, volunteers and conscripts, into the world's richest and most powerful civilization in three hundred years is a remarkable fact and myth of modern history, but the North American adventure was not for the faint-hearted. It required the confident stride of the active mood.

I grew up on an offshore island, whose culture was more circumspect. No one told me to go west, young man, because if I had, I might have landed up in the Republic of Ireland, which was officially neutral but notoriously sympathetic to Nazi Germany. In those days, we English were proud of our self-discipline. We queued: we did not barge or scramble. We tried to be respectable, that is, capable of being respected by others, which embraced more than just speaking or dressing in a respectable manner. To defend one's rights or to defer to a higher authority were both ways of being considered respectable.

The use of the active and passive moods reflected the lines of demarcation drawn between something that I did and something that was done to me by someone else. "I was taught French at school" has a different ring from "I learnt French at school". The first acknowledges the influence of my teachers, while the second sounds like a CV in which I am drawing attention to my own achievements. In their contexts, both could be polite, both could be correct, but the secret to being respectable lay in recognising the context.

All crowded societies are inflected with such nuances, which perplex the outsider and slow down the thought processes of the insider, until a modernising system comes along like Microsoft Word that standardises the active mood and downgrades the passive to the level of personal choice, and nobody needs to worry about how to be respectable. Modernity is frequently a process of simplification, but the details that are discarded may not be fussy or unimportant. They may reflect levels of authority, relationships, origins, aspirations and patterns of behaviour, which are often condemned as class distinctions. To ignore them altogether is like driving a motorway through an old market town. You may be able to get from one city to another more quickly, but only at the expense of the homes, family businesses and what Giddens might call the social "structuration".

A visitor who wanders through a market in New Delhi can quickly recognise the castes, religions and relationships in the turmoil of the stalls. In Northern Ireland, the sign systems marking the catholic and protestant districts are plainly discernible from the flags, murals and painted street kerbs. These are highly inflected societies, where democracy has had to take into account of the presence of deeply rooted and hostile cultures. When Marshal Tito took control in the Balkans after World War II, he brought the small but quarrelsome nations into one federation, which called itself modern and democratic, by breaking up their centres of power and imposing multi-culturalism by law. Each sign was written in five languages. Each ethnic group had its national theatre. But when Tito died, his Yugoslavia broke up in the fratricidal slaughterhouses of the 1990s; and Zagreb became the cosmopolitan capital city of a virtually independent country, Croatia, that it almost is.

In less crowded societies, such inflections are less needed. Where there is freedom to roam, there is more chance to escape.[13] This was one reason why the US, Australian and Canadian soldiers who came to Britain during and after the Second World War seemed so open in their manner – "over-paid, over-sexed and over here", as the saying went. Some came from places that were more crowded than my hometown, but they had inherited a myth of freedom that anyone with guts could carve out a future in a world where nobody fenced them in. In time, these distinctions moderated and merged. We relaxed and they became less brash. We learnt rhythm'n' blues, they played our kind of football and with that muddled slowness, which infuriated the Modernists about old Britain, we learnt how to get along with each other and to enjoy each other's company.

Something similar happened in Central and Eastern Europe during the 'years of stagnation', as they were disparagingly called. The last years of the Cold War was a time of slow adjustment, in which the threat of global war receded, but nobody wished to alter the balance of power too soon. Small UNESCO NGOs, such as the IATC, came into their own by arranging conferences, providing invitations to international events and exploring the widening cracks in the Iron Curtain. The queues lengthened at the crossing points where East met West in Berlin, as more families visited the other sectors more often. The weight of propaganda was heavy; the bureaucratic obstacles were still hard to overcome; but the countries that bordered the divide, such as Poland and Germany, came to know the strengths and weaknesses of the two political systems clearly and intimately.

It was in this region, rather than anywhere else, that the personal battles were fought that finally decided the fate of Soviet communism. In Britain, there were still too many left-wing fantasists, well-known playwrights among them, and when I first visited Poland, in 1977, before the rise of Solidarity, the only person I met who praised the communist system was an academic from the United States on a five-day, fact-finding tour. But in central Europe, those who wanted to visit their relatives or set up businesses on the other side tested the myths that supported the orthodoxies on a daily basis. They were the unacknowledged prophets, who brought about an end to the Cold War.

When the Berlin Wall came down, there was a rush to fill the ideological vacuum. In East Berlin, economic textbooks in their universities changed overnight. In Bucharest, streets were littered with four-page newspapers from political parties that had been in existence for at least three weeks. In Petersburg, where the old name of Leningrad could still be seen, the Len-Soviet Theatre for the Education of the Young was turned into a casino. Someone seemed to be painting a cartoon of the Free World across Eastern Europe, with gangsters, clip joints, whores, and massive posters everywhere; but, behind this display of free enterprise, the voice of the Orthodox Church could be heard once more, denouncing the greed and corruption of the Modern (and Western) world.

In Western Europe, steps were taken to transform the European Community (EC), which, after the Maastricht Treaty in 1992, became the European Union (EU). The Treaty recalled the "historic importance of ending the division of the European continent" and the "attachment to the principles of liberty, democracy and respect for human rights", while respecting the "history, culture and traditions" of its peoples. But some countries wanted to strengthen the EU as a federal structure. Others, like the British, distrusted the idea of federalism. The French treated the United States as its rival, while the British deferred to it as an overlord. Some Germans hoped that the EU would contain right-wing nationalism, while the Dutch pointed to the old Soviet Union and Yugoslavia as warning examples of what happens when such federations fall apart. But, on one point, all were agreed. It was far more difficult to find a suitable constitution for all the inflected nations of Europe than to federate the wide, open spaces of North America.

Britain was suspended between the active and passive moods, that is, between a US, which saw its role as the leader of the Free World, and a would-be United Europe (UE), which was resigned, if rebelliously, to being led. In either case, it could be no more than a junior partner with some influence but no authority. The only way in which Britain could make its mark upon the global stage was by setting a good example, the last refuge of the terminally respectable, or in Blair's phrase, by sending out a "beacon to the world".

Lighting up time would be at midnight on 31 December, 1999. The beam would point towards the Third Way and its lighthouse was the Millennium Dome.

The Dome began as an urban regeneration scheme. The site, Bugsby Marsh, was a stretch of the Greenwich peninsular where the outflows from old chemical factories and gasworks had penetrated the earth to a great depth. The Conservatives commissioned the architects, Richard Rogers Partnership, to design an exhibition space to attract tourists and re-vitalise a run-down area of South London. The project had cross-party support.

The Conservatives wanted the Dome to be run like a large village fair, in which every community in Britain could set up its own stall and the visitor could discover what a rich and exciting place Britain really was, a heritage proposal. New Labour preferred something entertaining but educational, where parents could take their children to find out how a modern world worked. The Liberals, as far as I know, had no official policy.

While its contents were still unknown, but subject to speculation in the press, the Dome came under attack. Its critics included senior bishops of the Church of England, academics, leader writers and economists. A well-known curator, Stephen Bayley, was appointed as its arts consultant, who resigned and wrote a book about his experience.[14] Its financial resources were supposed to come from funds set aside for millennium projects from the National Lottery and matched by private sponsors; but when its estimated costs rose above the limits of its known credit, some sponsors became wary and contracts were left unsigned.

The minister in charge, Peter Mandelson, denounced the critics as "sceptics" as if they were the scum of the earth. He visited Disneyland in Florida to pick up ideas on how to run a major tourist attraction, but came back to more bad publicity. Few liked the idea that modern Britain should be sold like Mickey Mouse. The chair of the New Millennium Experience Company (NMEC), a government-appointed *quango* that had been delegated to run the Dome, was Michael Grade, ex-BBC, ex-Channel 4, who became the chairman of the BBC's Board of Governors and soon left to become the Executive Chairman of ITV, the leading independent TV company in Britain. At a time when even he did not know what its contents would turn out to be, he dismissed two of the Dome's honoured ancestors, the Great Exhibition of 1851 and the

Festival of Britain in 1951, as class-ridden occasions in which "the great and the good created wonderful tableaux, then lifted the curtain and allowed the great unwashed to have a peep."

"This show," he claimed unwisely, "is different."

"Here the people themselves are the focus. The people are in charge. What the Dome says to them is: 'here you are, folks. Here are your choices. You decide." But the People, whoever they might be, were not in charge. They did not ask for the Dome or come to it in large numbers. The Festival of Britain was attended by about 18 million people in six months, whereas the Dome struggled to find 4.5 million visitors in a year. The Great Exhibition was better attended, funded privately (not publicly), offered ticket concessions *and* made a profit. But 'the people' only paid for the Dome by risking a flutter on a National Lottery, whose proceeds were distributed by *quangos* in a form of public expenditure that did not have to be approved by parliament.

But Grade's remarks expressed the Dome's message, the myth that New Labour wished to convey to the world at large. In the past, Britain had been a class-divided and racist society, but was now a united, multicultural family. It achieved this transformation through the effective use of market forces and modern management methods, the Third Way.[15] The best way to achieve the "greatest good of the greatest number", which was surely a goal of all left-of-centre politics, was through market research, efficient delivery and marketing. To that extent, 'the people' were in charge, as the customer was in charge (through market research) of a supermarket.

In 1997, Stephen Bayley suggested that they should all go away for six months to think about what the Dome was for and decide what it should contain. This seemed quite unrealistic. Sponsors had to be found, contractors hired, marketing strategies agreed, the press informed and everything kept within a tight overall budget. Six months spent on thought? What an "absurd", "naïve", "pretentious" and "frankly self-indulgent" idea!

Instead the NMEC split up the space within the Dome into a number of zones like departments in a multiple store. The first aim was to find sponsors for the zones, but some were more popular than others. Marks and Spencer backed the Self-Portrait zone, "a celebration of our country, our people, our attitudes and tastes, chosen by our people", where a mirror took pride-of-place. The City of London, centre of the financial market, and a consortium of City Interests, sponsored the Money zone, which told the history of coinage and the virtues of capitalism. Tesco, the supermarkets, sponsored the Learning zone and Boots the Chemists helped to finance the Body zone.

The Faith zone, first called the Soul zone, did not attract many sponsors. The Hinduja Foundation came to its rescue with £1.5 million. The Hinduja family was rich and influential, with interests in finance, communications and oil, and famous for its charitable benefactions, but three of the brothers faced charges of corruption over an arms deal in India and one was trying to obtain a British passport. In the nostrils of the sceptics, the gift had the whiff of a bribe.

The NMEC invited 22 teams from design and events management firms to bid for the "imaginative" side to the zones, whose contents were chosen through questionnaires and focus groups. The production director, Clare Sampson, gave the chosen teams a list of questions that someone in the street might be expected to ask. For the Body zone, they included: "Are we what we eat? Are there Seven Ages of Man? Can we feed the world?" For the Faith zone, they were: "What is the meaning of life? Is God dead? Can science find Him – or Her?" The teams were expected to research these questions and find out the answers from the experts. They were asked to embody the results in a visitor attraction that could meet the NMEC's operational requirements, such as budgets and estimated attendance figures of 5000 people per hour per zone. The teams were not expected to have opinions of their own. The leader of the Faith zone team was agnostic.

The Faith zone was always going to be controversial. A multi-cultural visitor attraction dedicated to Faith sounds like a contradiction in terms. After much thought, the design team settled for a tent-like structure in blue with a humming noise where visitors could sit and contemplate Infinity, a crèche for the soul. Outside the tent, there were some obelisks, giving the facts about the faiths. The one for Christianity stated: "Jesus Christ was born in poverty and died tragically young," which left the public to wonder what he might have achieved, if he had lived a little longer.

"Size does matter," cheekily suggested the souvenir programme that listed many "fantastic facts" about the Dome. "If the Dome was inverted under the Niagara Falls, it would take more than ten minutes to fill." It could hold "18, 000 double-decker buses". The New Millennium Experience was filled to the brim with similar facts. What it lacked were reasons why we should be interested in these rather than in a trillion other possible facts. What *can* be measured is fact. What we *choose* to measure is myth. The skill that went into the Dome's engineering was undermined by the naivety of its myths, which turned it unintentionally into a telling epitaph for the age of Modernity.

Some facts that were not included were more fascinating than the ones that were. It is still curiously difficult to determine the real cost of the Dome. The figures provided by the National Audit Office in November 2000 revealed that grants that totalled £628 million were given to the project, but this did not cover the money needed to keep the place free from vandalism when it was closed. The nearly final costs, as widely published in the media, varied from £750 million to well over £1 billion, a margin of error of 25%. Between £150 and £200 was spent for each person in Britain, whether or not they visited the Dome, but a family with two children would still have to pay an extra £100 to buy their tickets. For the same amount, the major churches could have been restored; every arts company could have been endowed with a trust fund to secure its independence from the state; or universities could have tripled the scholarships available to needy students. Indeed, there was no shortage of good causes on which to spend such a serious sum.

The Dome's supporters claimed that to spend all this money was not in the long run significant. The value lay in the reclamation of the land, but it proved difficult to sell the site. Eventually a £4 billion deal was struck with the Anschutz Entertainment group, a US-based company, but no money was exchanged. Instead Britain would receive a share of the profits, which were estimated to amount to £560 million over twenty years. Why was the real estate so hard to sell? According to Nicholson, the land was not fully cleaned in the rush to get the Dome ready for the Millennium. "Not all the contamination had been purged from the polluted ground of the old gasworks. Much of it was now sealed with clean crushed stone marked with an orange demarcation layer." This would last for about 25 years, when the poison would seep back to the surface.

For a year, government spokesmen protested that the Dome was a great success. Sir John Bourn, head of the National Audit Office, went out of his way to state that the "building and opening of the Millennium Dome in the very short time scale required was a tremendous achievement." Few bank managers under these circumstances would have sounded so supportive. Despite such help in high places, the Dome came to symbolise a government in a state of denial, quicker to quarrel with the truth than to admit it. After all the brave plans, the Dome seemed destined to become little more than a casino, operated by a company whose president was under investigation in the United States for fraud.

There is no reason to doubt the sincerity of its good intentions to marvel at the silliness of the New Millennium Experience, what waste of space, a lot of space. For one amazing day, it was amazingly expensive. It missed most of its targets, although it was driven by a kind of managerial obsession. Its contents were determined by hand-picked experts (and against the advice of other experts) and focus groups. The 'imaginative' side was kept apart from its contents, as if the imagination had nothing to do with reality, but only with presentation. As a taste of things to come, the 'Age of High Modernity', it was about as tempting as a frozen TV dinner; but in its managerial and political incompetence, it provided an unfortunate precedent for the next and even bigger state bonanza, the 2012 Olympic Games.

But at least one target was met. It opened on time. On the stroke of midnight, in the vast Millennium Dome, the Prime Minister, Tony Blair, crossed his arms and held hands with his wife, Cherie, on one side and Queen Elizabeth II on the other. They sang "Auld Lang Syne" to welcome the Millennium Year. Behind the Blairs and the Windsors were ranks of young people, carefully selected from all walks of life, races and creeds, crossing arms and holding hands, a happy and united family. The images were beamed around the world. It was the most expensive photo shoot in history, Blair's bid on behalf of Britain to make the first front cover of the twenty-first century.

Notes

1. Adam Nicholson: *Regeneration: The Story of the Dome* (HarperCollins, 1999).
2. Summer, 1989.
3. Samuel P. Huntington: *The Clash of Civilizations*, p. 91.
4. Ibid., p. 30.
5. Ibid., p. 91.
6. Henry Kissinger said that Huntington's *The Clash of Civilizations* was "one of the most important books to have emerged since the ending of the Cold War".
7. Notably in *The Shield of Achilles: War, Peace and the Course of History* (Knopf, 2002).
8. In Robert Harvey: *Global Disorder* (Constable and Robinson, 2003).
9. First published in 1995 and revised as *Global Disorder* in 2003.
10. By Faber and Faber. Mandelson and Liddle were two of Blair's close associates.

11. Ibid., p. 3.
12. Anthony Giddens: *The Consequences of Modernity* (Polity Press, 1990) Chapter V, p. 151.
13. In 1995, according to The Economist's *World in Figures*, there were 28 persons per square kilometre in the United States, 2 in Australia and 2 in Canada, as opposed to 239 in the UK, 229 in Germany, 5,612 in Hong Kong and 20,482 in Macao.
14. Stephen Bayley: *Labour Camp* (B.T. Batsford, 1998).
15. See Anthony Giddens: *The Third Way* (Polity Press, 1998).

Chapter Three
Two Thousand Five Hundred Years
of Modernity

There was no obelisk to Modernity in the Dome's Faith Zone, because Modernity was not thought to be a faith. Its authority came from science, logic and the observation of verifiable facts. A Modernist might have a faith as well, such as Christianity or Islam, which could influence his or her behaviour in non-objective ways, but Modernity was considered to be different from a religion in that it was based upon facts. If these were not available, it was honest enough to say so. If the missing facts were vital to form an opinion, it might institute a research programme or at least apply for research funding from the government, but the public could rest assured that the principles of science and accountability were being fully observed and that Modernity was not just a faith.

And yet in the eyes of many millions of people who were not brought up in the ways of Modernity, such claims were misleading or false. No less than other religions, Modernity depended upon assumptions that were unprovable, which revealed to its followers some aspects of reality that seemed so truthful and so appropriate for their needs that they responded in their hearts, "This is right!" The authority of Modernity grew over many generations. What began as a stimulating, philosophical proposal became a problem-solving and universal faith in its own right.

As its methods became better known, it attracted funding and political support, until it became institutionalised as the unacknowledged state religion of the West; and its influence spread further through normal empire building. It permeated the curricula at schools and universities, the agendas of the civil services and the feasibility studies at boardroom levels, until the doubters who questioned its validity ran the risk of becoming social outcasts. Too much was at stake to topple the house of cards by paying attention to the jokers in the bottom row. But the house might still topple.

Plato, the ancient Greek philosopher, whom medieval theologians treated with almost as much respect as if he had been a Christian, sowed the seeds of Modernity. In *The Republic*, Plato compared the state of human knowledge to that of prisoners in a cave[1] who could only guess at what was really happening outside from the shadows cast upon their cavern walls, but Plato's reality did not mean the temporal world, which was but a passing phase, but the essential forms from which all material objects were derived. Human beings were just imperfect copies of the 'Ideal Being' in the mind of God. Christians interpreted this to mean that he had anticipated the presence of an 'Ideal Being', Jesus Christ, before Christ was born, but that as a pagan, he could only rely upon the "shadows" that indicated His presence. But Christians had the example of Christ to guide them, the ideal made flesh.

In his collection of post-critical reflections, *Myth and Modernity*, an American professor of philosophy and religion, Milton Scarborough, described the impact made by the re-discovery of Plato's *Timaeus* in the early fifteenth century. In this Socratic dialogue, Plato discussed the theories of Pythagoras, a mathematician and musician, who had lived in the previous century and was thus one of Socrates' founding fathers, an eminent philosopher known and respected throughout the Greek world. Pythagoras argued that the material world could be expressed in the language of numbers, which proved to Plato's satisfaction that the laws of mathematics were ideal, not temporal.

According to Scarborough, "Copernicus and Kepler were ardent Pythagoreans and shared with Galileo the belief that the universe was made of numbers. To know what was true of nature, one only had to discover what was true of mathematics".[2] This extension of Platonism was harder to reconcile with the teachings of the Church. It drew Copernicus towards the conclusion that the Sun was the centre of our universe and Galileo to his trial by the Inquisition in 1632, where he proved with his telescope (although he was forced to re-cant) that Copernicus was right. Such debates with the Christian Churches lasted for many centuries, each constructing and de-constructing the other, in a process that continues to shape the culture of the West.

At a time of religious wars, when the authority of the Roman Church was being attacked and defended across Europe, the reasoning of such thinkers held wide appeal. Without openly questioning articles of Christian faith, another way of understanding what we mean by 'Reality' came into being, which did not rely upon how the Bible was interpreted. Scarborough attributes the rise of Modernity as a faith to Descartes, the French mathematician, in whose work the division of reality into "inner experiences and outer world received its definitive philosophical expression".[3] Our understanding of reality could be divided into "subject and object, private reality and public truth". Mathematics was the primary intellectual discipline with laws that could be studied to prove that some assertions were *objectively* true and not merely *subjective* intuitions.

Descartes, who died in 1650, was a pioneer in the practical developments that stemmed from the beliefs that came to bear his name, Cartesianism, that the material universe could be explained in terms of mathematical physics. He pursued the formal sequences of the scientific method: observation, mathematical analysis, testing and verification and conclusion. He developed analytical geometry and founded optical science. He influenced the generation of scientists, philosophers and mathematicians that included Leibniz in Mainz, Newton in Cambridge and Locke in Oxford – prophets of the Enlightenment, a pan-European movement. At the same time, what T.S. Eliot described as "the disassociation of sensibility"[4] took place that separated thought from emotion, observation from spiritual intuition, objectivity from subjectivity, and came to characterise the late seventeenth century and the Western epochs that lay ahead.

The changes that stem from the Enlightenment have permeated our minds so deeply in the West that it is easy to forget that its assumptions are unprovable. There are no numbers carved or planted in the world's crust. We place them there. There is no physical division in our brains between 'subjectivity' and 'objectivity'. These are two very useful ways of interpreting reality, but are not part of that reality, nor do they provide a comprehensive account. There are many aspects of human experience that cannot be explained in the language of numbers, which may be one reason why so many prophets of the New World Order were rather bad at guessing what would happen next. Like the myths from other cultures, those of Pythagoras and Descartes revealed aspects of Reality with such clarity and precision that we were drawn to believe that they were real in themselves, but if we altered the myths, we saw a different Reality.

The Cartesian mythmakers placed objectivity and factual knowledge before the spiritual disciplines that, according to many other beliefs, should go with them. The ancient Greeks established the rule whereby all medical doctors should take the Hippocratic Oath. Those who were taught about medicines and poisons were supposed to be committed by a sacred pledge to the saving of life, but those who learnt about human biology just from *Gray's Anatomy* might turn out to be tyrants and murderers. Science, it has been said, is without a conscience.

The myths that divided 'objectivity' from 'subjectivity' and factual knowledge from intuitive wisdom, often helped the compromises that had to be made with the Christian churches. Science and religion were both held to be authoritative, but in different spheres, one for fact, the other for morals and spirituality, following the lines of the Greek distinction between *logos* and *mŭthos*. Unfortunately, this separation diminished both causes. The churches could casually ignore the weight of experience and analysis that came from scientific research, sometimes (as in the case of AIDS) with appalling results. Their influence diminished as well. Even school biology classes could undermine the authority of a parish priest.

As religious thought became detached from factual knowledge, it lost much of its appeal for philosophers, but seemed to rejoice in its born-again innocence, as if too much mental reasoning might damage its spiritual integrity. Many Christian churches avoided awkward confrontations with the scientists by retreating towards the merely sentimental and by sticking to their old legends and parables, as if they alone were guides to good behaviour. The road to Hell is surely paved with *Thoughts for Today*.

The validity of the sciences, however, was also brought into question, for it is hard, if not impossible, to separate fact from myth. Even if we push our emotions and self-interest to one side, to study a phenomenon with an objectivity that satisfies our peer groups, we have still to choose the object of our research. If, as school-leavers, we decide to study medicine rather than physics, our choice will have been influenced by many unprovable factors, among them the extent to which we value life itself. If, in our minds, we elevate fact at the expense of myth, whatever we do is likely to rest upon arbitrary motives and shallow assumptions.

The main pitfall for Western science lay in its wishful thinking. It became so confident of its methods and results that it was tempted to create a model of reality, which conformed to its measurement systems, rather than the other way round. Life was expected to meet its targets and, if it did not, there must be something wrong with life. Plato's Idealism still casts a long shadow on the cavern walls of High Modernity, where earnest bureaucrats plot the next giant leap forward in human development.

The achievements of the Enlightenment thinkers transformed the societies in which they lived. They prepared the way for modern maps, publishing, dictionaries, encyclopaedias and the standardization of time. In 1676, the foundation stone was laid for the Greenwich Observatory, where an International Dateline came to be engraved. The features of modern Western culture slowly became recognisable, if still vague, including the industrial revolution, the market economy and democratic government.

Among his other accomplishments, the philosopher and mathematician, G.W. Leibniz, was a librarian and student of languages. A Christian who sought to reconcile empirical sciences with the teachings of the Churches, he believed that there was one perfect Language before the confusions caused by the building of the Tower of Babel. The perfect language should be logical and contain a comprehensive vocabulary that provided a clear word or sign for each known object or experience. He made up such a language from his misreading of *I Ching*, The Book of Changes, written in the third century BC by the legendary Chinese poet, Fu Hsi, and brought to Europe by a Jesuit missionary, Father Joachim Bouvet, in 1697.

In 1703, Leibniz published his *Explication de l'Arithmétique Binaire* in which he explained how a system composed of binary numbers, 0 and 1, could be extended to infinity to provide a symbolic language in which all knowledge could be listed and categorised. Unfortunately, as Umberto Eco has pointed out, it was socially unusable. This language was "no longer a practical social instrument but rather a tool for logical calculation."[5] It was nothing more than a form of cataloguing, but its future eventually lay in the machine language of computers, which allows them to be programmed in languages that we *can* understand; and this was, in itself, no small achievement.

Leibniz's binary language illustrated one limitation of Cartesian myths. They could become detached from normal life, but still sound very convincing, so that they could unsettle without being useful, an example of what Giddens called "dis-embedding". Those who were used to getting up with the sun and going to bed with the moon now regularised their lives by the arithmetic of the town clock. Dictionaries were standardised to provide a 'correct' spelling of words, pronunciation and grammar. They sought to offer a 'denotative' (rather than 'connotative') vocabulary, which connected a sign with what it was supposed to signify. Words were provided with one definition or several definitions, instead of letting them drift with imprecise meanings, as in the varied, allusive, many-layered and colloquial language of such pre-Enlightenment writers as William Shakespeare.

But the Enlightenment was not exactly Modern. "Enlightenment thinkers," according to Roy Porter, "felt driven to address the dynamics of change ultimately in terms of overarching visions of progress".[6] What the prophets of the Enlightenment held in common with Modernity was the assumption that the human species could be examined objectively, as if we could step out of the prison of our senses to see ourselves as we really were. The cutting up of dead bodies might frighten the superstitious, but it was the first step in scientific research for an anatomist. There was a nerve-tingling tension between felt knowledge, such as the fear of the dead, and analytical knowledge, such as a study of anatomy, which was one of the attractions of blood-bath melodramas and their modern equivalent, the Horror Channel.

The most formidable barrier for the Enlightenment scientists to cross, and a supreme example of "disembedding", came in 1859 with the publication of Charles Darwin's *The Origin of the Species*. Most previous thinkers had sought to reconcile their discoveries with Christianity, so that an orderly universe, which obeyed mathematical laws, was proof of a rational God, who favoured mankind, but the theory that human beings had evolved from other species challenged the biblical account of creation and the role of man in the divine plan. At what point did the apes cease to be apes and become humans with souls that possessed an intuition of God? Had God directly intervened? Or was this an old wives' tale that science had displaced with its superior knowledge?

What kind of consolation could the prophets of evolution offer those who were convinced by the logic of Darwin's theory but regretted the loss of the soul and the promise of redemption in an after-life? For some, it might be possible to keep science and Christianity in different parts of the mind, but others found this kind of co-habitation hard to handle. Thomas Huxley, "Darwin's Bulldog", invented the word, *agnosticism,* to describe the point of view of those (like him) who kept an open mind about God. But for those who threw aside their Christian faith, evolutionary theory offered a large compensation. By observing how animals evolved without divine intervention, a scientist could speculate on how the human species might have developed, if it had behaved differently. We could change our evolutionary path, and unchain Prometheus from the rock where the Gods had condemned him to suffer. Mankind may have lost its unique place within a divine plan, but it had gained a greater degree of influence over its destiny. It faced a future that, in some ways, it was better able to control.

Modernity was born from the marriage between Cartesianism and Darwinism; and rose to its maturity during the second half of the nineteenth century. Its youthful prime was in the 1890s, when the prospect of a new century and the challenge of the New World in the

Americas stimulated the imagination. This was a time for science fiction, colonial adventure stories, histories of the future, fantasies of space travel and giant schemes for the Betterment of Mankind, including socialism itself. In his preface to *The Golden Bough* (1890), Sir James Frazer, father of modern anthropology, described how mankind had evolved from magic and witchcraft, to religion, and on to science, which scattered other faiths in its wake. He expressed the mood of the age, the *zeitgeist* of Modernity, which was bold and competitive, but had not lost touch, as yet, with the open-ended spirit of enquiry in which it had been conceived. It was still flexing its muscles and wondering what new astonishment the exploration of the universe might bring.

Some cultures looked back to a Golden Age that they try to recreate. Others turned to Holy Scripture. European Classicism evoked the ages of ancient Greece and Rome. But Modernity always looked towards the present and the future. The past represented lower rungs on the evolutionary ladder. The peak of this process was always today, with the future as the goal to which it aspired. To balance this optimism, Modernity offered some awful warnings. A species could become extinct. It could fail to adapt or be defeated by alien beings in a war between the species. The survival of the fittest was the first law of nature. Humans had to obey that principle or suffer the fate of the dinosaurs, dodos and other lost or vanquished species.

But it was not easy to modernise. It meant making sacrifices for the good of the tribe or the species. Even the last General Secretary of the Soviet Union, Mikhail Gorbachev, is said to have believed that the massacre of the kulaks in the 1930s, which equalled the Holocaust in its senseless slaughter, was a necessary phase in the modernisation of Russia. Since the process was as ongoing and continual as evolution itself, it meant that life was a constant struggle to become something else. There was always a risk that, without such a struggle, other living organisms would take over and the world would become less under our control. Modernity was stressful. It was prepared to sacrifice the daily pleasures of life for the greater glory ahead, but sometimes those transitory joys included life itself.

For true Modernists, the progress of science and technology was irresistible, which was why Giddens called it a juggernaut. We all had to learn how to climb on board or perish beneath its wheels. It came to include such areas of study as the social sciences, economics and business management, which did not conform to the logical procedures that we associate with 'science', but had successfully imitated the outward forms of a science. But when Modernity seemed at its most unstoppable, it started to behave more like an old-fashioned religion, High Modernity. It could be dogmatic. Like any other faith, it gave the impression that it knew what reality was, and how to interpret it, and its followers were very puzzled and alarmed, as well as intrigued, when they discovered a detail that did not fit its general picture. It predicted the future. It wanted to make converts and, like the muscular Christians of a previous age, it was ready to intervene by force, if necessary, to correct the heretics and non-believers. It was bemused by other faiths, and tried to steer clear of them, but when it was confronted by myths that were not of its own making, it fell into a sad confusion. When it met with resistance, it tried to re-shape the world in its own image. In short, it turned fundamentalist.

Even in its prime, Modernity showed signs of its coming obsolescence. Early in the twentieth century, the Enlightenment myths upon which it was based came under scrutiny. In 1903, Bertrand Russell published *The Principles of Mathematics* where he set out to prove that mathematics was objectively true, but he came to the conclusion that it was only a branch of logic, a man-made invention. In 1906, Albert Einstein produced his *Theory of Relativity*, questioning the laws of the Newtonian universe. In Vienna, Siegmund Freud cast doubt upon the power of the rational mind to over-rule the greater strength of the libido, man's instinctive self, so that dreams were thought to be a better guide to human behaviour than manifestos.

He was supported by wave after wave of *avant-garde* artists, from Alfred Jarry in Paris and the Polish architect and dramatist, "Witkacy", in the 1890s to the Dadaists, Surrealists and the Theatre of the Absurd, each of which left their mark upon the billboards and the advertising screens. They all rebelled in their own ways against Thomas Huxley's "organised common sense", which was how he described the scientific process. Ferdinand de Saussure, the Austrian founder of Structuralism, dismissed the possibility that language itself was anything more than a game, like chess, which was driven more by its own conventions than by any direct contact with real life.

These sceptical views were important, but they were not, on a practical level, very useful. Bank tellers could still count, apples still fell from trees and it was still possible, despite Saussure, to accuse someone of lying, but the philosophical issues that they raised became more pressing when, after half a century of wars, revolutions, social change and yet more triumphs of technology, some people started to question whether Modernity was such a good thing. Most twentieth century Utopias were Modernist in inspiration, but they had an indifferent record of success. If Soviet Communism and National Socialism were discounted as aberrations of the Modernist spirit, this still left the welfare state and social democracy among its achievements. The tower blocks and concrete jungles might be eyesores, but, with the advances in scientific knowledge, the hospitals were better equipped and in the West, we were more prosperous and lived longer.

These extremities of triumphs and disasters pointed to the flaw in Modernity, the elevation of fact at the expense of myth, so that all the scientific achievements were unevenly matched with the casual notions as to how human beings should think and behave. We lived in an age of space travel and mass labour camps, with Silicon Valley on one side and Dead Man's Gulch on the other. In the depths of the Cold War, during the 1960s, the spirit of Post-Modernity stirred, whose sceptical eye surveyed the scene; and took the East and the West alike to task for pretending that its political systems were more reliable than they were and based upon principles that appeared to be immutable laws, but turned out to be nothing of the kind.

As its name suggests, Post-Modernity was not exactly against Modernity. It simply came after Modernity and accepted that the futuristic myths were man-made and fallible. It offered no alternative. Indeed, it could not do so, without falling into the same trap that had snared the Modernists, by claiming a super-human authority that it did not possess. To those who insisted that the future was something that they "can, and must, control", it could only respond with a sceptical smile, as if to say, "If you think you can, you might be able to do so!" Its skills mainly lay in taking apart or de-constructing the myths that other people had invented. It was good at de-mystifying language. By a kind of lip-o-suction that removed anything that sounded too abstract or philosophical from its vocabulary, language itself was changed to stress the idea that man was the measure of all things.

Most Post-Modernists despised notions of 'high' and 'low' art, the outmoded canons of taste that were based, in their view, upon ancient and corrupt hierarchies. Whole literatures were studied for the signs of gender, racial and class discrimination. University courses in what used to be known as the Humanities became attached to the Social Sciences. Morality became political correctness. Artists became cultural workers. History became 'heritage', that is, the kind of history that made people feel good or bad about themselves. In the US, many information officers now called themselves "perception managers". Rhetoric, the ancient art of persuasion, was vastly simplified, as slogans and iconic images turned out to be equally effective in changing people's minds. Even literary critics, I am sorry to say, abandoned the skills of their 2500-year-old trade, in favour of saying simply that they liked this or that in a sincere tone of voice, as if any loftier opinions might be thought to be politically incorrect.

Deconstruction was not just a tool in literary criticism. It was an analytical process with many applications, as much in the fields of fashion, life-styles and design, as in verbal languages. It could examine the nuances in inflected societies to get rid of many of them and standardise social practices in a way that went far beyond Microsoft's downgrading of the passive mood. The French Post-Modernist, Jean-Francois Lyotard, put forward the theory that societies were held together by 'meta-narratives' that gave priority to certain events,[7] but ignored others. The alternative histories of the French- and Anglo-Canadians (or the Catholics and Protestants in Northern Ireland) were examples, but so too were the legends that held political parties together, alumni associations and football teams.

But, according to Lyotard, in advanced capitalist societies, these 'narratives of national identity' were breaking down. They had been undermined by the free flow of trade and information across national borders – and by the need to accommodate many different faiths and ethnicities within the boundaries of the state. In the West, we were living in a Post-Modern world, whether we liked it or not, and a forward-looking government should acknowledge that fact. It should stay neutral, if possible, in the old-fashioned patriotic rivalries, but seek to construct a different kind of narrative, one more appropriate for an open society, which could bond with similar societies through a common belief in human rights, democracy and free speech.

Post-Modernity paved the way for Bobbitt's "virtuous circles", the Peace Process in Northern Ireland, the new EU Constitution and Blair's New Labour, but in getting rid of the old myths and inventing new ones, Post-Modernity was at a disadvantage. It could not claim that its ideas were 'true' in an old-fashioned sense. It was not a theory of knowledge, but of perception. If enough people believed that something was 'true', then it could be accepted as such and, if helpful, used as a touchstone for reality. If it conflicted, however, with the views of the government, or some other influential body, it could be easily discredited.

Language was prized more by what it did than what it supposed to mean. Advertising led the way. An image of a moon, a calm sea at night and a naked woman riding on horseback across a lonely beach may not seem a logical way to sell life insurance, but, on the level of the collective unconscious, its mixture of serenity and adventure might do the trick. Of course, an advertising campaign should never exactly lie. There were laws against misleading factual claims and it was bad publicity to be caught fibbing, but there was, and could be, no moral obligation to "tell the truth", as our parents and grand-parents might have wished. No language was capable of being "truthful". It was a social game, nothing more.

But it was a game that (after Post-Modernity) was being played to somewhat different rules. The skilled market analyst could find out, often by using focus groups, what words or signs triggered positive or negative reactions among the public or within a particular target community. By using the positive images rather than the negative ones, he/she could sell a product more efficiently.

Sometimes the product was a manifesto or a political party. When Blair came to power in Britain, he was supported by his team of special advisers, including Philip Gould, an expert on opinion polls, and Alistair Campbell, a former journalist for *The Mirror* who became his Director of Communications and Strategy in his government. They brought new marketing skills to the Labour Party that they had learnt by studying President Clinton's campaigns for the Democrats in the United States. They acquired the Democrats' latest software, Excalibur, to analyse trends; and borrowed many ideas from the Clinton style, his instant rebuttals, his ambiguous statements and his selective use of statistics.

They were not just selling a party. They were modernising democratic practices in Britain. It was effective campaigning, but was it (to use an old-fashioned word) very honest? Like George W. Bush, Blair was an avowed Christian. He was a member of the Christian Socialist Movement, with others in his cabinet, including his first Minister for Culture, Media and Sport, Chris Smith. When he was once asked by the BBC journalist, Jeremy Paxman, whether Bush and he ever prayed together, Campbell intervened to say briefly, "We don't do God!" Why not? Blair's faith might be expected to influence his views on many issues, but openly to talk about it on television risked negative publicity. He might alienate the Moslems, Hindus and Jews in a multi-cultural society, as well as losing the votes of atheists and agnostics. Faith was temporarily sacrificed for the television image.

In another age, Blair's Christianity might have been the first plank on his political platform. Instead, Modernity took pride of place. In the past, or so it was said, Britain had been an old-fashioned country that New Labour was set to "modernise". "I never said modernising the country was going to be easy," Blair wrote in his 1998 New Year's message to the readers of *The Mirror*, and many other papers at the same time, but in his early months in office, he often made it seem so. He sprang to the task of governing with the same zeal that he had shown in transforming the Labour Party.

But with his large majority in the House of Commons and a dispirited opposition, he looked less like a radical reformer and more like the leader of one of those task forces, to be seen nightly on television in do-it-yourself programmes, who could landscape a garden or convert the awkward little space under the eaves into a fourth bedroom in hours and come back next week with another set of bright but inexpensive ideas. Like them, Blair had a check list of promises, his strict budgets and timetables, his harmless old gaffer who could chip in with a tip from the days of yore (Michael Meacher, the Minister for the Environment in his first government) and his mandate for change, which kept the electorate, like the couples who drew the short straws in the *Changing Rooms* series, blindfold until the end, so that they could eventually gasp at the improvements to their lives, and marvel at the shades of lilac and magenta on the living room walls, before enquiring where exactly were the photos that used to be on the piano, and, come to that, where was the piano?

Culture was supposed to be a central feature of their modernising programme, if the arts and the media stayed (according to the minister for culture, Chris Smith) within New Labour's "overall agenda". That, however, was a big "if". If it simply meant that arts companies should obey the law and stay solvent, there was nothing too sinister about such a statement, but if it implied that the arts should accept, and conform to, the mixture of High Modernity and muscular Christianity that brought New Labour to power, it could become an intolerable restriction and lead to officious meddling.

Such a policy could mean that the mistakes of the Dome were repeated on an even grander scale. Or it might mean something like perception management. Like those medieval churches that painted visions of heaven and hell across their high roofs and lofty arches, Western airwaves might become dominated by the flowcharts, news flashes, polls and other measurement systems of High Modernity, each detail re-enforcing its beliefs. But it could be even worse than perception management. It could mean the construction of something like a state-sponsored virtual reality machine, which the late French Post-Modernist philosopher, Jean Baudrillard, might have called a 'simulacrum'. It might be convincing and, within its own terms, logical, but if you looked closely, you could see how the animated clones, which passed for people, responded to a limited numbers of commands and had little free will of their own.

Indeed, there was no shortage of apocalyptic visions, but at the heart of them all, there lay a paradox. Objectively, there might be little connection between the sign and what it was meant to signify. To that extent, language was nothing more than a game, but, subjectively, our aims in playing that game might be to tell the truth, however imperfectly, and to communicate that truth to others. Just as you cannot fully separate facts from myths, or objectivity from subjectivity, so you cannot detach the word from the motives of the speaker or the listener. All communication rests upon the assumption of good faith, even lying.

If we assume that language is merely a social game, whose only purpose is to manipulate public opinion or, worse still, to impose authority, it starts to deteriorate. We do not bother to speak it well or to listen to it carefully, except under threat. The slogan and the mission statement become literary genres in their own right. The jargon of business management buries its intentions beneath the crust of its defence mechanisms. Academics write to impress their peers in terms which only they can understand. We lose the mental discipline of language and, finally, the necessary links that connect words with what they are supposed to mean, crack and break, to expose great gaps in our efforts to understand the outside world, a process which, if taken to an extreme, would be the biggest "disembedding" of them all.

Notes

1. Plato: *The Republic*, Part VII
2. Milton Scarborough: *Myth and Modernity* (State University of New York Press, 1994), p. 11
3. Ibid., p. 10
4. In his essay on *Metaphysical Poetry*
5. Umberto Eco: *The Search for the Perfect Language* (Blackwell, 1995), p. 287
6. Roy Porter: *Enlightenment*, (Penguin Books, 2000), p. 230
7. See *The Post-Modern Condition*, a report for the Quebec Government, published in English by the Minnesota University Press (1979)

Chapter Four
Man at the Mercy of Measurement Systems

Every prisoner who entered the concentration camp of Auschwitz beneath its mission statement, *Arbeit Macht Frei* (work makes you free), was tattooed with a number. To many at the time, 1941, not only in Germany, this made sense, as did the policy of keeping the Jews, mentally defectives and homosexuals apart from the rest of the population, who were supposed to be fit Aryans. It was agreed that, just as there were inferior strains in the plant and animal kingdoms that should be weeded or culled to improve the species as a whole, so there were flawed strands in the human race. Social engineering on this scale required a systematic approach, hence the numbering.

The Final Solution, the euphemism for what became known as the Holocaust, required the services not just of psychopaths and serial killers, but also of normal men and women, who signed up to this programme of mass slaughter in the belief that they were serving their country. They took pride in obeying their instructions to the letter. Their ledgers were often models of tidiness. They could discuss the cost-effectiveness of one form of killing over another. It was their job. Somebody had to do it.

The numbers were useful in two ways. They helped to catalogue the inmates, so that each could be taken to work or the gas chambers in turn, and they also helped to remove the clinging inflections of former lives. A name implied a family, a job or a birthplace. A number had no such connotations. It signified no more than the presence of an objective being and its place within the scheme that the government determined. The numbers assisted the guards to focus upon the simple fact that this being had been brought to the camp, according to the orders of the authorities, and to stop them from being distracted by irrelevant or sentimental details, such as who the person was and whether he or she was likeable. It may have helped some prisoners too. By thinking of themselves as numbers, they kept the pains of family loss, rage and fear at a distance.

For some guards and inmates, numbers could be a kind of anaesthetic, but for others, they were more of a challenge. As a young man, the artist, Josef Szajna, was a member of the Polish resistance, arrested when he tried to escape to Hungary. He was sent to Auschwitz and the number, 18729, was tattooed on his arm. He interpreted this by numerical divination to mean that he would be "twice alive". He was eighteen, the first two digits, while the last three added up to eighteen as well. He was placed in a cell in the death block, but saved by what seemed like a miracle. The commandant at the camp was replaced and the new officer in charge commuted his death sentence to hard labour. His youth and fitness to work may have helped.

Numerology did not assist his escape, but this game with numbers may have helped Szajna in other ways. He found something to interpret as a lucky omen at a time when other signs of hope were gone. He humanised his serial number as a way of gaining some control over it, as we may choose our pin numbers by linking them with our birthdays. This helps them to be remembered and to seem more specifically ours. Under the de-humanising conditions of a labour camp, Josef Szajna was asserting his humanity against the regime. He did not resign himself to the thought that his number was allotted at random to assist the culling, but pretended that it had been chosen by hidden forces because of his age and destiny, an anniversary gift.

In his later life, Szajna called this "a metaphysical experience"[1] – both the loss of identity and the attempt to snatch it back again in this superstitious manner. If so, it is an experience that many share. Modernity encourages the transformation of people into numbers for easy cataloguing. Whether its aims are malignant, as in the case of Nazi Germany, or benign, as in the case of a welfare state, the popular reaction to it may be similar, at least in tone, some resentment and the sense of being demeaned.

If I fill up a form for a bus pass and am required to give my date and place of birth, my gender and ethnic identity, I know that these signs of my existence will be computerised and analysed statistically, from which god knows what inferences may be drawn. To a small extent, I lose control over my reasons for being. I may need the pass and be quite convinced that the boxes to tick will not be used for a kind of Final Solution, but be far less confident that the statistics will always be employed in a way that I would willingly accept. They might well mislead. And so even in filling up the form, I feel a little uneasy, as if a part of my life were being betrayed.

Some people may object to the way in which I have used the extreme example of the Holocaust to tilt the balance against Modernity or to imply that there is a kind of connection between such an atrocity and form filling. Numbers are just numbers. They are morally neutral. They cannot be blamed for the Final Solution nor praised for helping the treatment of cancer, but all Modernist states rely upon measurement systems, in which numbers are given an authority that other ways of expressing the human condition are held to lack. Measurement systems elect governments, provide balance sheets, grade students and assess the prospects for retirement pensions.

They are indispensable for most administrative purposes. They have taken over a role that in other societies is played by seers, gurus, oracles, prophets or witch doctors. They forecast the future. They have come to pre-empt the discussion about values that was once at the core of Jewish, Christian and classical humanist traditions. From the way in which the boxes are ticked on a bus pass form, demographic surveys may be constructed, which may influence political and commercial decisions, including employment and whether there are enough Asian women in parliament.

But some aspects of life are more measurable than others. Some may be impossible to measure. The rule by numbers focuses the attention upon those areas of human experience with which it can most easily cope. It anaesthetises emotions and feelings; and overlooks the wisdom, intuition and personal knowledge that may come from broader experience. It can be de-humanising.

In retrospect, the twentieth century, the Age of Modernity, seems singularly cold-blooded, the Final Solution heading or *not* even heading a list of similar atrocities. If we are encouraged to think of people in terms of numbers, the fate of one person seems much less important. But any one of us might be that person and so, although we may outwardly conform to the rules that are imposed on us, inwardly we rebel.

A hardened statistician, the supreme number cruncher of number crunchers, will acknowledge that all measurement systems have their limitations. If you know exactly what you want to measure, you can usually devise a system for doing so, but the trick lies in knowing what you want to measure. The US economist, Steven Levitt, has demonstrated[2] how misleading statistics can be, when allied to a political cause. He gave the example of crime statistics in the United States, used to attack or defend different methods of policing, from ultra-soft to ultra-tough. The results were contradictory and seemed to depend upon who was commissioning the research. He did, however, demonstrate that there was a link between lower crime rates and those states that had legalised abortion. When women were given the freedom to choose, they were more committed to looking after their children; and so there were fewer unwanted adolescents on the streets. His conclusion was that the measurement system was fine, provided that you could find the people to commission the right questions, which is why some other statisticians have proposed that this kind of social analysis should be left to robots and computers. But who programmes them?

The value of measurement systems to a Modernist society is that they seem to be objective: they can apparently settle disputes between subjective points of view. So much political weight rests upon the authority of measurement systems that time and money has to be spent on their continual improvement. Areas of experience that had once been thought to be beyond measure, such as the love of beauty, have new measurement systems devised for them. Wherever possible, the non-measurable areas of experience are made to seem of minimal importance or eccentric.

But to humanise the process, alongside all the efforts to improve its efficiency, there is the private temptation to make it worse, to foul up the system and to lie to the clipboard. Planned economies fail to work because there is resistance to the planning. A person may approve of the aims of the measurement systems, but in practice find ways to bend the rules to his/her personal advantage. Governments devise penalties for those who fail to fill the forms correctly or conceal relevant information, but we find ways to cheat the penalty systems.

The language of the forms vacillates between the legalistic and the chummy, in an effort to be clearly understood rather than vague, 'denotative' rather than 'connotative', and new systems have to be devised to calculate the degrees of error in the old ones. Forms are simplified or made more complicated to avoid the mistakes from creeping back into the systems of the future. They pile up in a dated order of precedence upon desks and databases, until the process suffocates through the efforts at improvement, and slowly succumbs to a death by numbers, and we all suffer, except accountants and lawyers. They seem to thrive.

As High Modernity started to behave more like a religion and less like a line of enquiry, so it sought to impose its authority upon more aspects of life. This rule applied as much in global corporations as it did to national governments, but the problem was not so much with their aims as with their measurement systems. Benevolent-sounding governments can be among the most bureaucratic. Some Christians defend their religion by saying that Christianity has never failed because it has never been tried and many communists say something similar. So do Modernists. The faults do not lie with Modernity, but with those who fail to fill up their forms correctly or who live in the past. But new measurement systems can be devised to isolate non-believers, so that the will of the Modernist majority can prevail, and the undecided can be persuaded to toe the line through perception management.

This faith in measurement systems cuts across party political lines. In Britain, a Conservative government introduced league tables for schools to promote parental choice. The aim was to introduce the rules of a market economy into a public service. How were the tables to be devised? Should schools be rated by academic standards, which might be unfair to schools with too many students from non-English-speaking backgrounds, or by mixing academic tests with other sorts, such as by introducing citizenship tests into performance ratings? Should schools, which had successfully grappled with the trade in drugs, be given a higher grade? In the United States, Levitt argued that such targets and league tables actually lowered school standards, because they encouraged teachers, as well as students, to cheat.[3]

The problems did not end with devising the tests. If too many parents favoured one highly rated school, would not other schools in the same district find it harder to recruit pupils? If highly rated schools were given more money and prestige, as *best-practice* schools, would this not add to the disadvantages of the second best schools? Might not the league tables impose a class system on state schools as divisive as the fee-paying system that they were supposed to replace?

Under New Labour, the Performance (or League) Tables were a responsibility of the DES (Department of Education and Skills), helped by subsidiary bodies, such as OFSTED (Office of Standards in Education), QCA (Qualifications and Curriculum Authority) and LSC (Learning and Skills Council). National Learning Targets were introduced for all primary schools in numeracy and literacy, which were followed by KS3 (Key Stage 3), another National Strategy, to promote four principles in the *best practice* teaching – *expectations, progression, engagement* and *transformation* – that OFSTED was expected to monitor.

Some of these aims, however, were rather hard to measure, such as *high expectations* or *strengthening motivation*. By using the methods to raise team spirit in corporations, such as *setting of challenging targets* and *programmes of professional development*, the intentions could be monitored, even if the results could not. Tests measured the effects of similar tests, leading to a glut of self-fulfilling prophecies. Some teachers complained that they were spending as much time in filling forms and attending courses in professional development as they were in teaching. In 2003, the DES published a report on Reducing Red Tape and Bureaucracy in Schools. This advised that 125 new measures should be introduced, and monitored, which required the services of another committee, the IRU (Implementation Review Unit), led by frontline teachers. This would advise the DES on how to reduce bureaucracy and cut out the red tape. New measurement systems were devised to test old systems that tested really elderly measurement systems, in a Modernist version of the ancient riddle, "Who guards the guardians?" But the myths that were really being tested were not the standards of students, but those of the politicians that introduced the systems.

A commonly accepted aim was to ensure that there was fairness of treatment to all pupils in state schools. The Conservatives sought equality of opportunity, while New Labour pursued "inclusivity". Both political parties wanted to redress what they perceived to be social injustices, although they would have defined them differently. These good intentions lacked the fixed points against which the various levels could be measured. Where was the 'Point Zero' from which pupils should start their academic race? Most academic disciplines have such defined points. Mathematicians should be able to count. Violinists should play in tune. No such tests can be devised for equality of opportunity or social inclusivity, for there are, and can be, no fixed points.

When an inadequate measurement system is imposed upon an accurate one, the mixture can corrupt them both. The attempt to devise a set of A-level results that was socially inclusive may have led to the resignation of one British cabinet minister, Estelle Morris, in 2002 and led to such havoc with the league tables that John Dunford, the General Secretary of the Secondary Head Teachers Association, denounced them all as "statistical nonsense".[4] In *Managing Britannia*, Robert Protherough and John Pick cited the example of Brian Fender, the Chief Executive of the Higher Education Funding Council, who wrote in a letter to *The Times* that the quality of university research could be measured by a simple mathematical formula.[5]

> *The research produced by academics in this country is among the best in the world. The number of times the work of UK researchers is read and used by other academics ('citations') per million pounds spent is the highest worldwide.*

Protherough and Pick commented: "That such citations, even in a publication of the highest academic quality, merely add to a numerical total, and not to qualitative appraisal, should be obvious even to the most compliant of managerial zombies".[6]

This may be so, but it is a measurement system widely used within universities as well as by external funding bodies. Academics are promoted through the number of their citations. It has led to its own kind of corruption, such as tit-for-tat citations and publication for the sake of citations, a form of self-publishing, whose aim is less to be read than to be noticed for having been written. A prodigious number of big, mad books are published for the benefit of a small and dwindling number of academic colleagues.

Fortunately, education is only education, something you can grow out of. It is rarely a question of life-or-death or, for that matter, parish-pump politics. These need, in a Modernist society, different measurement systems. It might seem to be ghoulish to have 'Performance Tables' for hospital trusts, based upon the ratio of deaths to admissions. Instead, in Britain, a star rating system was introduced, as in hotel guides, with five stars, based upon waiting lists, budgets and audits, and patient opinion polls, three non-medical but very measurable tests. But to meet the targets for the reduction of waiting lists, hospitals were tempted to release patients quickly or to admit those whose illnesses could be easily cured. Such systems missed the point of what they were supposed to be measuring, but this did not seem to matter, for they promoted Modernity as a management system, which was justification enough.

The monitoring of the parish councils required another measurement system. Tables and ratings went out, guides to conduct came in. It is a principle universally acknowledged, in public as in private life, that the smaller the budget, the more acrimonious and hotly contested are the ways of spending it. In the case of the 8000 parish councils in England and Wales, the budgets were usually small, although there could still be conflicts of interest among councillors as to how they should be spent. The Local Government Act 2000 sought to compile a register of interests in which councillors disclosed their businesses and properties within the parish, their properties outside it, and whether they had spent more than £25 on entertainment.

In 2000, New Labour established the Standards Board of England, which included lawyers, civil servants, councillors and accountants, with full-time ethical standards officers, to examine the cases. The board was expected to sit twice a month, but after two years, its chairman,

Tony Holland, objected that it was having to sit once a week to vet more than 3600 complaints, some of which amounted to little more than, "He called me a plonker!"[7] What was apparently needed was a sub-stratum of referral boards, to throw away the trivial and to focus the Board's attention on more important cases.

The establishment of parish councils was intended to give some independence to communities to run their own affairs, but the establishment of a national Standards Board took away some of this limited autonomy in a move that was meant to protect democracy.[8] There are elections to get rid of councillors, newspapers to expose conflicts of interest and laws against corruption. A democratic institution that has to be monitored by a government-appointed *quango* can hardly be called democratic.

Individuals have little defence against the authority of a Modernist state, apart from an inner sense of rebellion. We do not have the same resources. We are not in a position to quarrel with a research programme of a university department. If we are told with enough conviction that 35% of the population is schizophrenic, we often find to our surprise that a third of our friends are behaving in an odd way, although we may not know exactly what schizophrenia means. If we are told that the police force is or is not institutionally racist, we are encouraged to observe how it behaves in ways that we might otherwise have overlooked. We seek what we have been told to find.

We may hope as democrats that the facts have been observed and analysed in good faith and in line with the policies of the government that we have elected, but there is always a risk of self-fulfilling prophecies. A Modernist government will know what it wants to find out before it commissions research and a university will research within the terms of that commission, but not outside it. The published conclusions will influence our behaviour, because many people will take the findings to heart, and new measurement systems will be devised to prove that the assumptions were right. Life will imitate art and the circle is complete.

It will be freely admitted that where public money is spent, a government has a duty to monitor what has been bought and how well it is being used. Early Modernist states, such as the Soviet Union, relied upon simple statistics, but Western democracies have refined the processes, and computerised them, and made them more voter-sensitive, so that it is now possible for the state to handle masses of information about the daily lives of normal people in a way that would have astonished Marx, Stalin, Lenin and other would-be architects of development. Modern identity cards can be stamped with information about medical history, banking and criminal records.

The three goals of the Enlightenment – equality, material progress and the greatest good of the greatest number – are (in theory) no longer aspirations. The advancement towards them can be measured. But in return for spending our money on good causes, the Modernist government claims the right to monitor how well its aims are being achieved, a sensible idea, but one that draws it towards totalitarianism. To protect the society against paedophiles or terrorism, private e-mails can be scanned for suspicious words. DNA samples can be taken from those who have been suspected, but not convicted, of crimes.

From piles of statistical information at its disposal, a government can construct a model of how a society ought to behave, and where it does not, which Baudrillard might have called a 'simulacrum'.[9] These models are useful. Whole areas of social policy can be plotted, as if in a video game. While the vision of a joined-up government may never become a reality, the linking of public service databases with economic forecasts from the treasury can be illuminating, if we can rely upon the measurement systems. If the systems are un-reliable or partly reliable, but not wholly, a Modernist government is faced with the choice of abandoning the system or improving it, which may be a long-drawn-out process. Meanwhile, we put up with management by approximation.

The alternative is to pretend that the *simulacrum* is right and what happens in real life is wrong. With the help of the perception managers, a model of the world, according to Modernity, can be imposed upon the confusions of daily living. We are expected to conform to it, rather than the other way around, perhaps with serious consequences if we fail to do so. Beneath the fig leaf of an electoral mandate and with the help of information technology, a Modernist democracy can out-snoop, out-pry and out-monitor a police state.

In *False Dawn*, John Gray, a Professor of European Thought at the London School of Economics, has described how a Victorian experiment in social engineering grew into a global *simulacrum*. The aim of *laissez faire* was "to free economic life from social and political control and it did so by constructing a new institution, the free market, and by breaking up the more socially rooted markets that had existed in England for centuries…" As a result, "a single world-wide civilization [would emerge], in which the varied traditions and cultures of the past were superseded by a new, universal community, founded upon reason".[10] Fukuyama and the Neo-Cons in Washington broadly share this view, but, as Gray pointed out, "the United States today is the last great power to base its policies upon this enlightenment thesis".[11]

The realisation of this vision "is the over-riding objective today of the trans-national organizations such as the World Trade Organisation (WTO), the International Monetary Fund and the Organisation for Economic Co-operation and Development". Led by the US, the West supports such institutions, whose aim is "to incorporate the world's diverse economies into a single global free market." But Gray concluded that "this is a Utopia that can never be realised: its pursuit has already produced social dislocations and political instability on a large scale. . . ."[12]

It is not hard to find a 'more socially rooted market'. In most towns and cities in the United States and Britain, there are still small businesses, which are owned by local families, who started them and handed them on, generation by generation, and whose names can be found as mayors, councillors and benefactors in the records of honour displayed in town halls. Such family businessmen realised that philanthropy and trade went hand in hand and that a reputation as a Scrooge or a Gradgrind put off their customers. But their numbers dwindled, as they failed to meet the challenge of the supermarkets and big corporations. Their family companies declined in size and they became more peripheral to the Western economy as whole.

Further afield, in Asia, the Middle East and India, markets are socially rooted to a great depth, which, according to many who believe in the free market, is mainly what is wrong with them. They are not free in a Western sense. They are surrounded with petty restrictions. The development of the economy is held back by the loyalties and corruption of their un-modernised societies, which may be inflected with racial, sexual and religious bigotry. But there is another side to this story. This informal trade sometimes moderates prejudice. It offers a good reason for not hating your neighbour. Extended families can provide a social security system and, sometimes, when a job needs to be done, someone, who seems to be working on his own, can summon up a whole army of cousins and nephews to help him. Miracles happen daily.

Among the traders, who travelled from China to Turkey on the ancient Silk Route, 5000 miles, a good family name was a priceless social asset. It was a passport, visa and credit card, rolled into one. A member of the family, who brought discredit to the family name, was ostracised, and even handed over to the police, for all travelling merchants needed to be trusted. It is still possible, as it has been for centuries, to buy Korean *kim chi* in the markets of Tashkent, as you can buy Uzbek silk trimmings in the streets of Seoul. This trading system has survived wars, revolutions, fluctuations in the value of many currencies and threats from mountain bandits, but it rests upon nothing more substantial than family honour and reputation.

A modern bank could provide many of these services, but not all of them, and it is not easy to change something like family honour into rules that can be applied to anyone, wherever they come from, whoever they are. Such a financial system needs to have access to a large database of personal records and a legal system, which pursues the defaulters. These require the technology and bureaucracy that many non-Western countries do not have. When some free market practices are imposed upon a "socially rooted" market, the effect can be to unravel the myths that bind the society together, like pulling at a stray strand of wool in a sweater.

What are seen in the West as the free market crimes of bribery and nepotism may be the driving forces of many socially rooted markets, and a Western company or aid agency that seeks to stamp out such corruption is drawn into the complex questions of how people actually behave in non-Modernist societies. A local businessman may be asked to handle a large aid budget, but is warned that he cannot use bribery or employ members of his family. He would be faced with an intolerable dilemma. Did he want to be rich or a good husband? If he did not give gifts to those in authority, what sort of businessman would he be? Bribery might be the only source of income on which his government could depend.

Under these circumstances, Western companies and charities start to pull away from the developing societies, which they are supposed to be helping. They may be physically isolated in compounds, like imperial enclaves, although they may not be richer in a material sense. Some aid agencies live monastic life-styles, although some private companies compensate their staff for not living in the West by paying them huge salaries. But, rich or poor, the companies and the charities share many Modernist beliefs. They don't like barter: they prefer hard currency. They don't like shamans: they do trust Western doctors. Nor can they necessarily be blamed for doing so, but the myths of Modernity create the secluded districts for Westerners, whose inhabitants provide the information for the databases that help to compile the big mad books, which provide the global models as to how the free market is supposed to behave.

Global financial institutions reflect and magnify these odd beliefs. They draw their information from international companies, naturally so, rather than from the cost of food in the local markets. This can provide a distorted picture. One country might be thought to be rich, after striking oil, though its crops may have failed and its population starving. A trader on a stock exchange floor may be able to calculate the impact upon a national economy that can be caused by a shift in the price of copper, but still not fully appreciate how this might be translated into a weakening currency, higher prices, unemployment and social disintegration. The measurement systems of the stock exchange may influence, but rarely accurately reflect, the transactions of the street, for a local market is usually closer to the real economy than a *simulacrum*

"The collapse of the global market place," wrote the financier, George Soros, "would be a traumatic event with unimaginable consequences. Yet I find it easier to imagine than the continuation of the present regime".[13] But in the English-speaking West, it is still easy to accept the myth of the benefits to be gained from a global free market, because we have not felt the consequences of what has happened elsewhere. In most respects, a *simulacrum* is more convincing than real life. It behaves logically. It fits the known facts. It predicts a future that 'we can and must control'.

That is the fatal attraction of most measurement systems. We want to believe in them, because they confirm our faith in Modernity. We are puzzled and disturbed when they go wrong; and our faith can be so strong that we prefer to ignore what we experience in favour of trusting what we invent. This is where the real damage occurs, not only in the wide world of global economics, although that may be serious enough, but also in the internal world, where we think about ourselves. We value a book for its sales figures, a CD for its place in the charts, a school for its league table rating, a hospital for its waiting lists, a government for the size of its majority and a life-span for its impact upon actuarial calculations. We become measurement junkies.

Notes

1. In an interview with the author, published in *The World & I* magazine, July 2003.
2. In *Freakeconomics*, written with Stephen J. Dubner (Allen Lane, 2005).
3. Ibid., p. 19.
4. *The Daily Telegraph*, 3 April, 2003.
5. *The Times*, 4 May, 2001.
6. Robert Protherough and John Pick: *Managing Britain* (Imprint Academic, 2002), p. 44.
7. *Daily Telegraph*, 24 February, 2003.

8. Tony Holland, the chair of the Standards Council, defended the process like this: "There is no doubt people are becoming so cynical about politics generally that if you don't do something the whole thing will just collapse."

9. See Jean Baudrillard: *Simulacra and Simulation* (University of Michigan, 1994).

10. John Gray: *False Dawn: The Delusions of Global Capitalism* (Granta Books, 1998), p. 1-2.

11. Ibid., p. 2.

12. Ibid., p. 2.

13. George Soros: *Soros on Soros* (1995), p. 194.

Chapter Five
The Trouble with Artists

During the 1990s, the little library of the Arts Council of Great Britain (ACGB) was filled to the brim with surveys, manifestos, working party reports, modest proposals and utopian visions. Apart from the ACGB's own publications, and those from the Policy Studies Institute, the Gulbenkian Foundation and similar bodies, there were leaflets from the National Campaign for the Arts and the main political parties, which published their own proposals, very often. They came from most shades of the political spectrum, including the Liberals, Liberal Democrats and Greens, but they were preoccupied with one main question. How could the needs and values of the arts be better accommodated within the requirements of a Modernist bureaucracy?

How could the social benefits from the arts be calculated? What sort of targets and measurement systems quantified success or failure? The language of the arts manifestos reveals the extent of the struggle. It contained portentous but vague words, such as 'Heritage', 'Identity', 'Accessibility', 'Accountability' and 'Diversity', borrowed from politics and the social sciences, which left the impression that you could not start a music society in Taunton without pledging to reform the world.

According to one commentator, arts centres *sanatised* neighbourhoods,[1] and made the streets fit to play in. According to another, Robert Hewison, the arts provided the "shaping moral medium" within which every other social activity took place. While these claims may not have been exactly untrue, they closely resembled snake-oil politics, and raised the question as to why, if the arts were so important, a government should bother to waste public money on anything else.

Without more rigorous guidelines, one civil servant, J.T. Caff, feared that the government would be pouring money into a 'Black Hole'.[2] But it was very difficult to devise such rules and regulations without cutting out too many deserving cases. In 1982, the Parliamentary Select Committee on Education, Science and the Arts decided to take a long hard look at arts patronage. It turned for its definition of the arts, not to

European neighbours, such as France and Germany, which were thought to be over-generous, but to the United States, which was supposed to be more philistine. It unearthed this sentence from the US National Foundation for the Arts and Sciences:

> *The term, the arts, includes but is not limited to music (instrumental and vocal), dance, drama, folk art, creative writing, architecture and allied fields, painting, sculpture, photography, graphic and craft arts, industrial design, motion pictures, television, radio, tape and sound recordings, the arts related to presentation, performance, executive and exhibition of such art forms, and the study and application of such arts to the human environment.*

This was less than helpful. Did all motion pictures count as art, even a surveillance video? If not, what was the difference between film-as-art and film-as-not-art? How did industrial design-as-art differ from the horrors of the mills?

In the US, these were mainly questions for the tax authorities to decide, but Britain was torn between the system of state patronage which prevailed in Europe and the American way of doing things, in which the market was supported by tax breaks, sponsorship, grants from foundations, private patronage and cable companies in dire need of something to put on their subscribers' screens. Most British arts lobbyists, however, looked towards continental models. They admired the *maisons de la culture* in France, the art collections in Italy and Russia, and the opera houses in Germany. There were two legendary precedents, the Greek and Roman examples, the Jekyll and Hyde of arts patronage. In the former, ancient myths – part history, part-religion – were re-visited and re-considered in open public performances; while in the latter, spectacles of cruelty and glamour were staged to entertain the mob: the small difference between feeding the soul and feeding the lions. In modern Europe, some countries have ministries for Culture and Religious Affairs, such as in Romania, while others have 'bread and circuses' ministries, where culture is treated as a leisure activity, like sport, gambling and general entertainment.

Meanwhile, in Britain, subsidy levels continued to rise. Despite the warnings of cuts, the Arts Council's grant grew from £62 million to £171 million under Mrs Thatcher, and almost doubled under Major's government, with an additional source of funding from the National Lottery, and reached about £500 million (apart from what was spent on the Dome) in 2003, under Blair, which was not a black hole, but heading downwards in that direction. But the demands from the arts lobbyists did not seem to lessen at all. Indeed, they seemed to increase, as more anomalies crept into the system and more good causes were found to justify the spending of more public money.

In the mid-1980s, to obtain a definitive answer to what was really needed, the Arts Council funded a National Arts and Media Strategy. The authors approached as many people as possible that were working in the arts and the media for their views, and the result was a very long shopping list, whose imaginary costs were outweighed by its imaginary social benefits. Its mission statement began: "The arts and culture are at the core of citizenship: they are central to the individual in society and national life. The challenge is to ensure that the arts survive! ". This naturally cost a lot of money.

Against such a chorus of special pleading, it seemed almost in bad taste to point out that the arts do not always spread sweetness and light. In Northern Ireland, during the Peace Process, bright murals were painted on the end walls of the terraces of Belfast and Derry. They showed cartoon-like figures, edged in black, carrying flags and rifles. The slogans were catchy and rhymed: "Trimble will Tremble, When the Boys Re-assemble." There could be a flourish of the art schools about them – "in-yer-face" scene painting for an "in-yer-face" age – but for those who worked and shopped in these streets, it must have been like living in the shadow of the gunmen.

Nor was it necessary to possess a long historical memory to recall that some state-funded cultures can be very repressive. Hitler and Stalin were profligate tyrants. They built opera houses like people's palaces, but drove dissident artists out of town, when they did not kill them. The old Soviet Union, unlike the United Kingdom, had laws prohibiting censorship, but it had laws against subversion as well. The arts were supposed to be free, but all activities that undermined the state were banned, which amounted to draconian oppression. A lot of faith in liberal democracy was required to believe that no Western government would ever travel down that road again.

In 1995, an arts columnist, Robert Hewison, who became an Oxford professor, published a book, favoured by the Arts Council, *Culture and Consensus*, in which he put forward his view that the country had become a "disunited kingdom", where "the broad post-war consensus of opinion" had begun to "break down entirely". "It is the function of consensus," he wrote, "to agree the terms in which a nation sees itself.

The breakdown of consensus leaves a nation with a weakened sense of its own identity".[3]

"Ultimately," he argued, "the culture of an individual, group or nation is not merely an expression of personal, collective or national identity. It *is* that identity. It follows that a nation's culture is not merely a private matter nor a marginal public responsibility, but vital to national existence." For this reason, he concluded that "the state has a responsibility to nurture and protect the work of artists and that may well call for subsidy and the calculation of economic return". Sadly, governments were not always as generous as they should be towards the arts, which must compete with other demands on the public purse, such as the social services, and "for too long, those for whom art is important have indeed allowed the defence of culture to go by default".

To complete this sales pitch, angled towards New Labour, he added a party-political message. He blamed Mrs Thatcher's government for the neglect of the arts, for she saw the "notion of consensus as an obstacle to progress" and "undermined many of the civil institutions, such as the BBC, which had originally been developed to administer and create consensus." When New Labour came to power, Chris Smith MP, the new Minister for Culture, Media and Sport, sounded very sympathetic. "The cultural life of the country was not an optional add-on to the process of governing", he said, "but a central feature of what makes for a good society".[4] Culture "helps to shape our sense of identity, as individuals and as a nation."

Some might think that Culture was acquired through a process of study and refinement, and helped one to appreciate the finer things in life, but Smith made it clear that the way in which he was using the C word, and by extension New Labour, was part of a spectrum that included the so-called 'high' and 'popular' arts. They could both be good in their ways, Elgar and the Spice Girls, and both contributed to a sense of national identity. Like Hewison, Smith had a hot line to the British psyche. The mourning at the death of Princess Diana was proof, he suggested, that the British were capable of "genuine emotion".[5]

Under New Labour, culture would be at the centre of government, with a seat at the cabinet table, if the arts stayed "within its overall policy agenda", and to prove that this aspiration was not just windy rhetoric, he set a target of "300, 000 new chances to experience the arts" in his departmental survey, *A New Approach to Investment in Culture* (1998), but ran into difficulties. How do you rate a new *chance* to experience the arts? Who would count them and why? Smith's collection of essays,

Creative Britain (1998)[6] , amused some critics in the press, for why should someone with his gifts waste them on the arts? And what had the arts done to deserve him?

But Hewison's argument, politically speaking, was a seductive one. What government could refuse the chance to "create and administer consensus" through its cultural policy? If effective, it would be an easy way to govern. What government could turn down the opportunity to promote "the shaping moral medium for all society's activities"?[7] But a thin dividing line separates such ambitions from manipulating what the public is supposed to like and dislike, using the powers of censorship, subsidy and perception management to do so, and once this border is crossed, we are into the realms of Big Brother and thought control – and the country that may beckon as a Utopia, but usually turns out to be another wasteland.

The word, art, is derived from the Latin *ars*, which meant *to join* or *put together.* "Hands, do what you're bid," wrote W.B. Yeats, "Bring the balloon of the mind, That billows and ebbs in the wind, Into its narrow shed." He was thinking about the act of writing poetry, but this brief verse applies to all the art forms, as well as to some languages, like mathematics, which were once included among the arts but are no longer so. All artists seek some suitable container for the balloon of the mind.

Yeats's "narrow shed" could be a medieval Memory Theatre, an architect's drawing or a poem, but the process is similar. Without finding an appropriate shape or form, it is hard to concentrate on any part of our experience, or even to think at all, but every imaginary out-house has its limits. There is always something that refuses to be pulled or pushed into it. The shed itself may be of the wrong size or shape. It may need to be re-built. The experience, insight, perception, what you will, may be elusive. It may seem to hover slightly to one side of our normal lines of sight. We may know that something is there, but be unable to see or touch it. We have to construct a new form for it. That is where the struggle begins.

Another word, *Artisan*, a manual worker or craftsman, comes from the same Latin root, but it acquired another meaning. At one time, the two were more closely bound together. All artists were considered to be craftsmen, who earned their livings by selling their skills to their clients, like the Greek poet, Semonides, who, according to legend, was the first paid, professional artist. High on the list of their services was persuasion. If it now seems strange that such different skills as landscape painting, playing a musical instrument and writing poetry should be lumped together as "the arts", it may be useful to remember that they were all once servants of Apollo, the god of oratory. It was one of their duties to persuade.

There was considerable rivalry among the various professions as to which was the most effective at persuasion, the musician who could stir feelings of love or war, the painter who spoke to the eye or the poet.[8] The words of the Bible might be sacred, but perhaps an image of the Mother and Child was more likely to move the congregation. The sound of music was said to be more seductive than the sound of words, but many orators claimed that rhetoric was pre-eminent among the arts, because it spoke to the mind as well as to the heart and the senses. It could persuade people to take action – and was thus the art of the politician and the military leader.

During the fifteenth century, the artist-craftsmen acquired a new status among the Italian city-states. Leon Battista Alberti was an example. He was a trained lawyer, a mathematician and classical scholar, and was employed by the Papal Chancery in Rome to write biographies of the saints in elegant Latin, but he chose to become an artist. He was a painter, as well as an architect and town planner, whose book, *Della Pittura*, described the mathematics that lay behind the illusion of perspective. If he had been just a craftsman, he might have wanted to keep this knowledge to himself, but he was more of a theorist and philosopher. He wrote in the vernacular to be more widely studied, a man with democratic sentiments.

The artist, who had learnt the rules of perspective, was capable of producing a three-dimensional image upon a one-dimensional canvas, which Alberti considered to be the most important skill in painting. The aim was not to trick the client, but to train the eye to see the outside world in a more sophisticated way. It added a spatial awareness to the information that a painting could provide. This changed a painting's composition, so that the eye could be drawn towards the focal point but still be aware of other details that contributed to the overall effect. Alberti was primarily concerned with the geometry of perspective, and how objects seemed larger or smaller in space, but Leonardo da Vinci, who was born when Alberti was in his late forties, carried his investigations a stage further by seeking to understand why objects seemed to change colour in space, so that green hills turned blue at a distance.

Alberti's rules of perspective quickly influenced painters throughout

Europe, although it still astonished many observers. The younger Holbein delighted in using perspective to produce sinister *trompes d'oeuil*[9], and Shakespeare commented upon its power to create illusions more than one hundred and fifty years later. *Della Pittura* provided artists with a grammar and syntax for their visual languages; and influenced the study of optics, at a time when Copernicus was putting forward the theory that the sun, not the earth, was centre of the universe. No telescopes were then available.

Like other intellectuals of his time, Alberti saw no distinction between science and the arts. That kind of apartheid came in with the Enlightenment. Da Vinci and Michelangelo were designers of military fortifications and inventors of war machines, as well as painters, poets and sculptors, and, with others, they embodied the spirit of enquiry that characterised the Italian Renaissance. One sign of this advancement was the presence of the new Academies in the Italian city states, to which artists might belong. As craftsmen, they would be members of a guild, which protected their trade secrets and legal rights, but, as Academicians, they were expected to devote their lives, like philosophers, to the pursuit of knowledge.

This caused controversy. Their critics argued that the skills of the artist, such as perspective, were always meant to deceive. The churches were vehement on this matter. Artists who illustrated the truths of the Bible, without ornament or distortion, might be said to be fulfilling God's will, but as independent philosophers, pursuing their own lines of enquiry, they were deliberately spreading errors and falsehoods. The Elizabethan noble and poet, Sir Philip Sydney, absolved poets in general from lying on the grounds that they never pretended to tell the truth. But they flattered, exaggerated and compared their lady's skin to satin or something equally fanciful. How could this kind of activity, which never even claimed to be truthful, be confused with the pursuit of knowledge?

The answer lay in form. Artists were not claiming to be creative, in the sense in which God created man, which would be heretical, but through their various skills, they educated the mind and the senses to see the outside world more clearly. Perspective was an example. Once the artist and his clients had learnt its rules, they were less likely to be deceived by optical illusions or, rather, while still not being deceived, they could enjoy the games of perspective. A room could acquire a sylvan vista, a park a more ambitious scale and a portrait a palatial setting.

Perspective was such an attractive device that it took several centuries before artists got out of the habit of using it and discovered the joys of the flat canvas again. The same might be said of other ways of training the senses, such as classical tonality in music. If the ear and the mind had learnt the scale system, a person could recognise and identify certain sounds, reproduce them and play games of harmony and counterpoint with them. In the eighteenth century, it had an added attraction. It was a way of organising sound that could trace its origins back to Pythagoras, who was a musician, as well as mathematician and philosopher. Counting the vibrating beats within a note, essential to tuning, could be regarded as an objective measurement system, a test of which even Plato, who distrusted all artists, would have approved.

Listening to music was thus placed, through tonality, within a philosophy and a history. But the process was two-way. Artists, while studying the models, re-invented them, so that the public understanding of the ancient world was influenced by how they chose to play by the rules or to break them. When tonality started to seem too small a shed to contain all the noises that musicians wanted to cram into it, they defied Pythagoras, and changed the rules, and used cracked notes and dissonances that he and his disciples would never have tolerated. By that means, musicians enlarged the range of sounds that we could pleasurably hear and so, in a small way, expanded our aural universe. Creativity is more a process of discovery than of invention.

The artists' primary tools are myths, not just stories but the assumptions that we bring to the interpretation and shaping of our experience. In their work, artists are continually promoting certain myths, and changing others, and discarding a few more. They are trying to build the better shed – which is where the social benefits from the arts mainly lie, not so much in promoting good causes, but in stimulating the flexibility of mind that can recognise a good cause from a bad one, and sifts out the living values from the dead or dying ones. But they may not succeed. They may accidentally knock the dunny down and be at a loss to know what they can put in its place. Sometimes that shed might not be just a games room or a cupboard for old rackets, but the system of beliefs that binds a society together. The ideal cultural policy would encourage a flexibility of mind, for this is how civilizations evolve, but discourage the arbitrary demolition of those myths on which the society depends. But that is a very delicate balance to maintain.

In March 1985, I was invited to give a paper to a conference in Moscow on "The Social Role of the Theatre Critic".[10] I had my lapel badge, my typed pages in an inner pocket and knew what I, as an IATC Vice-President, was expected to say. But I was determined not to say it. The General Secretary of the Soviet Communist Party, K. Chernenko, expressed the aims of Soviet cultural policy, like this: "the real extent of the influence that literature and arts on the whole exert on the moulding of the ideological and moral frame of the people's mind is the most precise criterion of their success",[11] which was exactly the kind of politically correct judgement that Soviet critics were expected to deliver. But my first response was something like "Nuts!"

It was too ambitious, too Modernist, and to a Western liberal with an Anglican Protestant background, it was shocking that a government should even try to "mould" the 'Mind of the People', as if it were putty. In my view, the social role of a theatre critic was to tell the truth, like everyone else, "although to say so out loud risks the charge of simple-mindedness"; and I went on to defend Free Speech in a high-minded way, calling it "Truth", waiting to be contradicted. I expected to be told that, in the West, free speech was something that sold newspapers and, if it did not, my "truth" would turn out to be nothing more than hot air; and so the debate would proceed along the familiar Cold War lines. But nothing like that happened, quite the reverse.

Those few days turned out to be momentous in the history of the Soviet Union, Russia and the world at large. They began with the announcement of the death of Chernenko himself, the last of the old Soviet leaders, who may have been dead for days, and they included his state funeral. A long line of Soviet officials stood on the balcony overlooking Lenin's tomb in Red Square, as the gun carriage passed. Soon most would be forgotten men, mourned by none but their families. By the end of the week, the name of next General Secretary of the Soviet Communist Party was announced, Mikhail Gorbachev, a man from a younger generation, less battle-scarred, and, almost at once, it seemed that the mood in Moscow began to change.

Wholly upstaged by these great events, and in the ancient capital of Russia, St. Petersburg, which was then known as Leningrad, a play had its opening night at the Maly Drama Theatre, *Brothers and Sisters*, based on a novel by Fyodr Abramov, and directed by Lev Dodin. It told the story of what one village in northern Russia, Pekashino, had endured during fifty years of war, famine and corruption. It pulled no punches. It demonstrated how Soviet *apparatchiks* were bribed and how the villagers had only managed to hold on to one cow for a special feast. All their other produce was sent to Moscow and they were on the verge of starvation. They heard the cheerful farming statistics on radio, watched the films of girls showing off their equipment on tractors, read the days-old editions of *Pravda*; and their disbelief turned to laughter.

The book was an epic, conceived in the tradition of Tolstoy and Solzhenitsyn, scrupulous with facts but imbued with a feeling for moral order and spiritual values. Its title was ironically derived from Stalin's first public address to the nation, after Nazi Germany attacked the Soviet Union in 1941. On the stage, the play ran for nearly seven hours, but there were long queues to see what had soon became a locally unmissable event, beyond anything that we might call in the West a smash hit.

All but one of the men in the village had been killed in the Great Patriotic War – or so it seemed. A woman, Anfisa, was head of its collective farm. Some months after the war, Anfisa was told that there was someone in the village square, who was asking for her. She did not recognise him at first and then could not believe what she saw. He was her lost – and presumed dead – husband. The Leningrad audience began to sob, at first quietly and then in waves of anguish. It was as if they were all mourning for their lost wives and husbands, their children and parents, buried in ice-bound graves, under bombardment from the Nazi guns.

Brothers and Sisters was not polemical, but as an account of village life under communism, it went beyond the anti-government documentaries and satirical plays of the West, far beyond, for example, David Hare's *Stuff Happens*. It was, on one level, a scathing criticism of Soviet bureaucracy and, on another level, like a moral witness. When it toured festivals in the West, it was received as a fine example of Gorbachev's *glasnost*, 'openness', and the fact that it was allowed to tour at all was certainly a sign of the times. But the way in which it had been brought into being had little to do with *glasnost*, for it was conceived, written and rehearsed during the Years of Stagnation, at a time when most Western observers believed that Soviet artists were groaning beneath the weight of censorship and political repression.

But the situation was far more complicated. Much had changed since the days when Boris Pasternak was denounced as "a pig that fouled its own sty" for writing *Dr. Zhivago*. There were unofficial underground theatres to which the authorities turned a blind eye. There was much *samizdat*, self-publishing, and many productions, adapted from Shakespeare, "our contemporary", which, for example, cast a Stalin look-alike as Richard III. In Moscow, there were well-known rebels, like Yuri Lyubimov, whose Tanganka Theatre could be compared to the Royal

Court in London, anti-government but not exactly anti-the-system, from which they both benefited.

Small theatres, such as the Maly Drama Theatre,[12] were given more license than larger ones, and there were rivalries between the central Ministry of Culture in Moscow and its regional outposts, such as in Leningrad. There was more flexibility in the system than seemed possible at a time when, if a Westerner wanted to meet a Russian friend, they would probably arrange to meet by accident in a public park.

At first, the idea of staging such a controversial book was dismissed by the authorities out of hand, but Dodin persisted. He was, as a point of aesthetic principle, scrupulously accurate. Much as the nineteenth century Russian landscape artists sat out in the cold and snow to capture the light on the bark of a tree, so he had taken his company of young actors to this very village, where they not only could observe the people concerned, but could work with them as well and get to know them as friends. This kind of realism had little to do with photographic reproduction. It was more of a spiritual quest, in which the actors sought to identify so completely with the villagers that they thought as they thought and acted as they behaved.

In this enterprise, they were supported by the Stanislavski-inspired training that they received through drama school, which sought to develop the imagination, not as fantasy or as an escape from reality, but as a way of understanding the human condition. This search was part of the rehearsal process, its very core, but it was not undertaken for the sake of popularity, still less for political reasons. Dodin could not be certain that the play would ever be staged, although he discussed each objection in detail with the authorities,[13] but he could summon up the ghosts of Dostoievsky, Tolstoy and even Maxim Gorki to support his case. They too had fought to tell the truth in difficult circumstances, but perhaps the most telling witness in Dodin's favour was not a person at all but the *zeitgeist*, the spirit of the times, for much of Russia, it seemed, was engaged in a deep and anguished soul-searching.[14]

This won the day, not only for Dodin but also for Gorbachev, and even in that conference room in Moscow, where the serried ranks of theatre critics sat with their pencils sharpened, the very word, "truth", seemed to have acquired a new weight. If I had started my paper by talking about "free speech", they might have looked at their watches and politely left the room. "Free speech" might mean anything – chatter, gossip, froth. Only in the West, under the High Street branch of Modernity, was it sometimes taken for granted that the way to truth led through the market place of opinion, just as the free market was supposed to lead to economic prosperity.

But the assembled few had a different respect for the word, "truth", which, in Russia, was associated with a spiritual and intellectual discipline. You struggled to tell the truth. You had to be educated. You had to know something of history. You needed to have a good vocabulary. You had to retain that self-control, which helped you to detect the truth, though every bone in your body was tortured and aching. You needed to be something of a martyr and something of a saint. You needed to be an artist.

"The idea of the arts as a kind of religious cult," said Dodin, "was always strong in Russia".[15] He instilled into his young company, many of whom had been his former students, a kind of aesthetic Puritanism. They were expected to train like athletes, to study like research students, to train their senses to pick up the vibrations from the outside world, and to develop their imaginations, so that they could feel their way into the lives that surrounded them. Each performance was an outer sign of the inner and open-ended search for truth.

But how could such a company fit into Chernenko's or anybody else's cultural policy? It was very difficult. On one level, you could argue that *Brothers and Sisters* did exert an influence on the "moral and ideological moulding of the People's mind", but, unfortunately, this was almost wholly to the disadvantage of the state. Whereas communism taught that the private family should take second place to society at large, *Brothers and Sisters* expressed almost exactly the opposite point of view.

In that case, would it have been better, if Dodin had been living in the West and enjoying the luxury of free speech? This was also hard to imagine. In the Soviet Union, Dodin had inherited a theatre that received a low but reliable grant. This gave him a degree of freedom from box office pressures and the demands of sponsors. It enabled him to hold his company together at a modest level, while they toured internationally for extra cash. Would a Western producer, however well intentioned, have accepted a state of affairs in which the performances were expected to change, night after night, to maintain the flow of improvisatory freshness?[16]

After twenty years, their situation did not change. The company still occupied its small but ageing building, and still toured for more money. In the meantime, the Maly Drama Theatre, despite its size, was recognised as one of Europe's leading theatre companies. "Theatre of Europe" was now attached proudly to its name.

There were those who said that if he had been more co-operative in his approach, if he had learnt how to market the company properly and network with the right sponsors, his company could have been living in a palace. If he had been more sympathetic to the requirements of Russia during *glasnost* and *perestroika*, he could have been appointed to one of the highest artistic posts in the country. He should have learnt how to fit in with the demands of the state's overall policy agenda and discovered how to mould the minds of the people in the way that, according to political correctness, it should be moulded.

Should he have compromised? It would have been a difficult decision, but if he had taken it, he would have been a different man and the Maly Drama Theatre – Theatre of Europe – would have been a different company, completely different, and even Russia might have been different, less rigid, less top-down and more welcoming of change. That is the trouble with artists.

Notes

1. This was an argument put forward by the Canadian sociologist, David Cwi, who pointed out that areas with arts centres in them had few examples of vandalism. But jazz was once associated with low-life, before it became gentrified. Raves and discos have a similar reputation today.
2. Mr Caff was speaking at a conference at the Edinburgh Festival in August, 1979. See John Elsom: *The Big, Grey Patch* (Contemporary Review, January, 1980).
3. Robert Hewison: *Culture and Consensus* (Methuen, 1995), Intro. xvii.
4. Quoted in *The Guardian*, 12 January, 1998.
5. Chris Smith: *Creative Britain* (Faber and Faber, 1998), p.16.
6. Published by Faber and Faber, 1998. The title echoed a similar book: *Creative Australia*, written by the former Australian Prime Minister, Paul Keating.
7. Robert Hewison: *Culture and Consensus*, Introduction, p. xiv.
8. An echo of this debate can be found in Shakespeare's *Timon of Athens* – Act One, Scene 1.
9. As in his painting, known as *The Ambassadors*.
10. This paper was published in *Contemporary Review*, May, 1985.
11. See John Elsom: *Cold War Theatre* (Routledge, 1992), p. 75 *et passim*.
12. "Maly" means small, but it was not a little theatre in a Western sense. It seated about 500 people.
13. I describe this process in *Cold War Theatre* (Routledge, 1992), p. 83-4.
14. In 1984, before Chernenko's death, I made two programmes for the BBC from Novosibirsk and Moscow, and was struck by the independence of such fringe theatres as the Theatre South-West in Moscow.

15. Lev Dodin: *Journey Without End* (Tantalus Books, 2005), p. 16.
16. In 2005, I interviewed Lev Dodin during a tour of the Maly Theatre's production of *Uncle Vanya*, which received superlative reviews, but his company was still rehearsing during the afternoons of the tour, still changing textual emphases and even actors.

Chapter Six
The Irish Peace Process

A peace process is not a peace agreement. It is almost the opposite of one. It starts from the assumption that the sides are so far apart that there is not much point in looking for an agreement, but only for some general rules, which may lead to an agreement, or, if this is still too optimistic, to guidelines that may lead to an agreement to differ. Myths, other than those of Modernity, are shunned, like creatures from the Black Lagoon. Questions of right and wrong are pushed to one side. Instead, the peace processors try to persuade all the parties to accept the will of the majority, measured by polls and electoral systems, upon which a model of good behaviour can be constructed. Instead of confronting myths to see what they contain, a peace process buries them beneath measurement systems, and unlike an agreement, a peace process has no time limit. It can be prolonged, indefinitely.

"The aspirations of people the world over are the same," wrote Senator George Mitchell in his memoirs, *Making Peace*. "To satisfy those aspirations they need work. Good jobs. Good paying jobs."[1] The young lads in Belfast who joined the paramilitaries sought the "steady pay and status that they [could] not otherwise achieve." The first step on the road to peace was to raise the level of prosperity. *It's the economy, stupid!*

To believe that more or less everyone wants the same sort of thing, whoever they are, wherever they may be, is a very large and useful Enlightenment myth. It combines a Christian faith that all are equal in the eyes of God with the attempt to analyse mankind objectively as a species, *Homo sapiens*. What began as a war cry against class privilege ("Men are born free but everywhere they are in chains") became the political *sine qua non* for the liberal welfare state. It divides and unifies political parties, unites the United Nations and is enshrined as a principle within many national constitutions.

It may be desirable as a principle, but it is, of course, unprovable and, at first sight, highly unlikely. Clearly, people do not always have the same aspirations. Mitchell explained that mothers and fathers need "to satisfy the economic needs of their families", such as education and health care, but not everyone is a parent and even economic needs differ. "They also have to be able," he added, "to satisfy their own emotional need for productive work, for self-respect, for meaning in their lives". But one person's productive work may be someone else's vandalism, and my *self-respect* may be your *pride* and his *intolerable arrogance*. *Meanings in life* have been known to differ as well.

All myths, however well intentioned, have darker sides. The reverse side of the coin of equality is that differences of faiths and cultures are of lesser importance, mere opinion, and if the material needs of a society are satisfied, other sources of discontent will wither away. Global managerialism rests upon such myths, so full of common sense, so fair-minded, suitable for a Modernist paradise where faceless thirty-somethings stride to work through sunny parks and cityscapes, as if in a brochure for an American MBA program or a trailer for John Birt's BBC. Only by looking at the details (or their notable absence) does the hollowness of the exercise become apparent, a parody of the human condition for can-do optimists, which leaves many questions unanswered. What work? What education? What self-respect? What meaning in life? And which of the many possible journeys from the cradle to the grave is right – or, at least, slightly better?

Mitchell was the senate majority leader for the Democrats in the early years of Clinton's presidency, the architect of win-win deals. When he retired in 1995, he was appointed to be the president's Secretary of State for Economic Initiatives in Ireland, an unusual position, for the US government has no jurisdiction over any part of Ireland, north or south. Through President Clinton's powers of persuasion, the Irish and British governments welcomed Mitchell as a mediator in their disputes over Northern Ireland. He submitted his report to the governments in 1996, which became the basis for the 'Good Friday' or 'Belfast 'Agreement, signed in 1998 and approved by public referendum. He was the principal architect of the subsequent Peace Process.

After the Cold War, successive US governments saw the role of the United States as the sole remaining super-power to be that of a peacemaker. The United Nations could not be so. It was too divided and lacked the necessary resources. Echoing Fukuyama's *The End of History*, President Clinton said in 1994: "Freedom's boundaries now should be defined by new behaviour, not old history – democracy every-where, market economies everywhere, countries co-operating for mutual security everywhere. We must guard against the lesser outcome."[2] The globalisation of trade and finance, the Internet and the spreading of liberal democracy around the world were all parts of this grand plan.

But Northern Ireland was an irritating piece of grit in this particular oyster, a region where democracy had not brought peace, and history refused to die. Sometimes, the dislike flared up, sometimes it calmed down, but, sadly, the voting systems seemed to have little to do with the levels of violence. To judge by the loss of life, the Troubles in Ulster rank very low indeed in the list of the world's mini-wars. According to the Royal Ulster Constabulary (RUC), 3210 people were killed from 1969 to 1996, of which 2260 were civilians, including paramilitaries from both communities. One independent study[3] attributed 1684 killings to republicans, 983 to loyalists, 318 to the British army and 53 to the RUC, but this was less than half the number that had been killed in traffic accidents in Ulster. The average annual number of murders, 10 for each 100, 000 members of the population, was less than in New York, Los Angeles or Holland. But comparisons were often made in the press with South Africa under apartheid, Chechnya under the Russians, and Bosnia, where 2,250 people were killed in two months in 1992 and 700,000 made homeless. The differences in scale should have warned that such parallels were absurd, but the Irish habits of mind always seemed to magnify the facts – the notorious M.O.P.E (Most Oppressed People Ever) syndrome.

A peace process of sorts had continued for decades between the Irish and British governments; and there had been unofficial meetings between the British government and the Irish Republican Army (IRA), which was reputed to have the largest private army in Europe, financed by Irish-Americans through NORAID, supplied with arms from Eastern Europe and blessed as "freedom fighters" in the Vatican's paper, *L'Osservatore Romano*. The IRA had links with organisations in Europe, Middle East and Latin America, and collectively they posed the threat of a terrorist network, similar to that of Al'Qaeda.

Straightforward elections, instead of solving the dispute, went straight to the heart of the problem. In a united island of Ireland, the unionists would always be in a minority, whereas in Northern Ireland, nationalists would always be out-voted. Since the two points of view were linked to religious faiths, Protestant and Catholic, as well as to the opposing narratives of history, neither was prepared to give way on the question as to which of the two states was the more legitimate. But a model for a possible future settlement slowly and tortuously evolved through such diplomatic summits as the Sunningdale Agreement in 1973, the Anglo-Irish Agreement in 1984 and the Downing Street Declaration in 1993, each of which failed, but left behind a residue of mutual understanding, at least between the Irish and British governments. Elsewhere, it often spread false hopes and alarms.

It was broadly felt that a settlement should consist of three strands – an Assembly in Northern Ireland with a power-sharing executive, an agreed formula that would allow this executive to meet the Irish government to discuss matters of common concern, and a British-Irish forum. This package should be put to the people in both parts, separately, for it was agreed (according to the Downing Street Declaration) that "it was for the people of the island of Ireland alone, by agreement between the two parts respectively, to exercise their right of self-determination, on the basis of consent, freely and concurrently given… to bring about a United Ireland, if that is their wish." The decision as to whether Northern Ireland should become part of the Republic of Ireland or stay within the United Kingdom would thus be left to the people to decide, after these bodies had become established.

These strands were carried through into the Belfast Agreement, although they all had to be negotiated in detail, but there was still a nagging problem – the matter of arms. In 1994, after the Downing Street Declaration, the IRA announced a cease-fire, which was matched by the loyalist paramilitaries, but the cease-fire did not mean disarmament or an end to the war. And yet how could democracy function, if political parties, like Sinn Féin, still had private armies at their beck and call? To insist that the IRA disarm might seem like demanding its surrender and so the British government looked for a phased *de-commissioning*, which might consist of three stages: an agreement in principle to disarm, an agreement on the practical measures to secure verifiable disarmament and the actual de-commissioning of some weapons "as a confidence-building measure".[4]

But Mitchell was among those who did not believe that the IRA would disarm peacefully in the wider interests of democracy. In the United States, the giving up of guns had a different resonance than in the UK. US citizens had a constitutional right to bear arms, whereas the British did not, not even their police. If at this stage, the US government had stood shoulder to shoulder with the British government on disarmament, the process might have taken a different course. But Mitchell was sent as a mediator instead. He persuaded the political parties to endorse six "principles of democracy and non-violence". They had "to renounce for themselves, and to oppose any effort by others, to use force, or threaten to use force, to influence" the peace talks. The onus was upon political parties that had links with the paramilitaries, like the IRA or the UFF (Ulster Freedom Fighters), to persuade them as well. They had "to urge [them] that punishment killings and beatings [must] stop",[5] and so end the intimidation of the sectarian ghettos.

The unionists argued that these principles still gave Sinn Féin too much room to manoeuvre. Sinn Féin could claim that it had done its best to persuade the IRA to give up its weapons, so that its delegates could take part in the peace talks, but the IRA might still not have left one gun at the door of the saloon. The British government agreed with the unionists and the IRA retorted by breaking its cease-fire. In 1996, it bombed Canary Wharf, London, killing two people, and blew up the centre of Manchester. It blamed the British Prime Minister, John Major, for these atrocities and argued that *he* had impeded the peace talks. The gulf between the two sides seemed unbridgeable. The real challenge, according to the nationalist (SDLP) leader, John Hume, was how "to de-commission the mind-sets," or, in other words, a matter for cultural politics.

When George Mitchell first came to Belfast, he sat with President Clinton to hear the leader of the Democratic Unionist Party (DUP), Dr. Ian Paisley's "thirty-minute recitation of the history of Northern Ireland from a unionist point of view . . . a fascinating story, well-told, totally one-sided and yet persuasive if the listener knew nothing else." They then listened to the Sinn Féin leader, Gerry Adams' "fascinating" history from the nationalist point of view – "well-told and also persuasive" – and wondered how it was possible to have such different views of the same society.

These histories were not opposites by accident. They had been crafted like that, as in some family quarrels, for it was rare to hear a nationalist point of view that could not be quickly countered by a unionist one, for the cultural tradition between them, polished to perfection, was that of mutual antagonism. If a nationalist asserted that Catholics were treated like second-class citizens, a unionist would reply that some Catholics deserved to be so, if they harboured terrorists and undermined the state, but, in fact, they received fair treatment. They could vote through a PR system and were, numerically speaking, over-represented in the British parliaments at Stormont and Westminster. But they were still in a minority. That's democracy.

If a nationalist quoted Sir James Craig, a Prime Minister of Stormont in the 1930s, as an example of Protestant bigotry, a unionist would point to Eamonn de Valera, the US-born former Taoiseach of Eire (the Republic of Ireland), who was prejudiced to the point of outright fascism, or mention the "special position of the Holy Catholic and Apostolic Roman Church" in Article 44 of the 1937 Irish Constitution. If a nationalist reminded anyone who was listening of Bloody Sunday, a unionist would retort with Bloody Friday. If a nationalist went back further into history by citing the Easter Rising or the Famine of 1847, a unionist would talk of the Somme or leapfrog back to the Battle of the Boyne.

Each side had its own historical narrative, each its heroes and victims. Each had its own streets, murals, slogans and colours – green and orange. "Each side's as bad as the other," the poet Seamus Heaney ironically remarked, "never worse." He himself was defiantly green.[6] Mitchell, plunged into the peace talks, must have been bewildered at the skill with which the war between the two cultural traditions was waged, the command of history, the erudite quotations, the theology and the brave sorties to seize the high moral ground. To listen to Paisley and Adams, one after the other, must have been like umpiring a Wimbledon Final, having just mugged up the rules of tennis in a taxi to the courts.

Which was more factually accurate? It was hard to tell. Both sides vacuumed up facts, and inhaled them in vast quantities, to clear the way for the triumph of their myths. But the facts were plucked out of context and if a mediator tried to track down the details, such as who fired the first shot on Bloody Sunday, an enquiry could drift on endlessly (as it did) and absorb the time and money that might have been better spent on investigating other tales of wrong-doing. To get out of the problem of having to choose between two causes, the British government under Major devised a policy of *parity of esteem* between *two cultural traditions*. But this proved to be more complicated than it sounds.

It led to a bureaucratic nightmare. All companies had to prove that they offered equal opportunities to Catholics and Protestants, whether they received public contracts or not. The arts were subsidised according to their affiliations rather than on their merits. Three government departments subsidised the West Belfast Community Festival, Féile an Phoail, which was no more than a Sinn Féin carnival. There was an insidious problem. 'Parity of Esteem' helped to institutionalise bigotry. It supported those who played the ethnic identity game, and discouraged those who were agnostics or preferred to seem less confrontational, such as the peaceful and hardworking Ulster middle-classes.

However eloquently they spoke, Paisley and Adams told less than half the story, for across the wide counties of Ulster, Catholics and Protestants lived side by side, and lent each other their lawnmowers, and the construction and de-construction of their myths went on peacefully, as it does elsewhere, through games, gossip and marriages. As Mitchell observed, "the beautifully manicured lawns" of Queen's University were "a more real part of Belfast than the bombs".[7] Much of the violence that gave Ulster its reputation was not so much between the two communities as within the sectarian ghettos, as gang leaders imposed their discipline upon those who strayed towards tolerance.

The way forward lay in recognising that all versions of Irish history, as with other 'grand narratives', were myths, which did not mean that they were untrue, but that they had been constructed to illustrate insights that were widely trusted and believed. "Perhaps the greatest of all difficulties," according to *The Leader* in 1904, an Irish nationalist weekly, "which underlie the whole of what is known as the Irish revival is the length of time that we are obliged to go back before we arrive at any mode of life that may in truth be termed distinctively Irish".[8]

D.P. Moran edited *The Leader*, a journalist from Waterford, who worked in London for ten years and joined the Gaelic League in 1896. He wrote *The Philosophy of Irish Ireland*[9] in which he distinguished between political and cultural nationalism. Political nationalism was a constitutional arrangement within the British Isles, in line with Gladstone's Home Rule, a Protestant construction born of an imperial regime, but cultural nationalism was something more profound, an alternative understanding of life, imbued with Catholic and Gaelic values, hostile to Anglicisation in all its forms.

The Leader represented a strand in Irish nationalism, which might be called fiery and fundamentalist, were it not for Moran's casual admission that "Irish Ireland" was not somewhere that could be found on earth. It had to be constructed. It was popular with the Irish abroad, such as Irish-Americans, who wanted to re-live the War of Independence. Because its aims were not limited to independence or Home Rule, it could freely gather up any sticks with which to beat the British. It supported de Valera's Fianna Fáil party, "soldiers of Ireland", in the 1920s and attacked unionists and Protestants, the "sourfaces", in the north. Moran kept a sharp eye out for "evil" literature, which was anti-catholic, anti-the-Irish-Irish or might subvert the new Republic of Ireland, Eire.

Moran's "Irish Ireland" was a pastoral country (unlike Britain), where families lived in happy and God-fearing communities (unlike

Britain) and spoke Gaelic, which was supposed to be a richer and more ancient language than English, although so few people (due to British imperialism) spoke it. Greening the Emerald Isle was a common pursuit of Irish writers in the years that followed the Easter Rising in 1917, partition and the Irish civil war. It was a cause that united W.B. Yeats, an Anglo-Irish Protestant, and Moran, who quarrelled with Yeats. As well as reviving Gaelic, which became the official language of the state, there was a revision of history, a rescuing of Celtic legends and a sniping against the British for their empire, class system and one-sided sense of fair play.

Moran's "Irish Ireland" owed a considerable debt to continental writers[10] of the Romantic Movement, who were inspired in turn by an eighteenth century German critic, J.G. Herder. Herder passionately disliked the Enlightenment and put forward the view that there was a mystical link between racial integrity and tribal territory, so that the spirit of the Folk was thought to emanate from the landscape it inhabited. "Have not all nations", Yeats once remarked, "their first unity from a mythology that marries them to rock and hill?" The Irish word, *dúchas*, expresses this idea. No English word matches it. It roughly means "roots", "the place of one's birth" or an "inborn nature". He, like Moran, defended the spiritual insights, supposed to be part of their unique Celtic heritage, and associated them with territorial integrity. This drew them towards other nationalist movements on the continent of Europe, the Third Reich and the big mad politics of the 1930s.

To students of Irish history who had watched peace initiatives come and go, the Belfast Agreement was another well-meaning effort to settle the dispute without actually coming to a decision. The aim was not to propose a settlement, which might have brought more violence, but to devise a process through which the differences of faith and opinion in the province could be expressed, which might lead in time to a new constitution.

"We acknowledge," ran the Declaration of Support, "the substantial differences between our continuing, and equally legitimate, political aspirations." It was ambiguous, deliberately so, although it was signed by all the political parties. If this preamble meant that the aspirations were equally legitimate as *aspirations*, it was an agreement to differ, nothing more. If it meant that they were equally legitimate as constitutional settlements, there was a problem with logic, for they could not both be *equally* so. One precluded the other. That was the problem, the one issue that had to be decided. At the heart of the Belfast Agreement lay a political vacuum, disguised by a display of fine and honourable intentions, but it would be unfair to suggest that the Emperor had no clothes. In fact, the reverse would be nearer the mark: all clothes, no Emperor.

The Belfast Agreement was sold to the people in Ireland, north and south, with a firework display of superlatives. It was a "truly historic opportunity."[11] Nationality, according to the Irish columnist, Fintan O'Toole, was now a matter of choice, "not of an inescapable destiny". "At long last," said the British Prime Minister, Tony Blair, "the burden of history can start to be lifted from our shoulders". In London, the BBC changed the term that it used for people who bombed hotels and supermarkets from terrorists to paramilitaries, which sounded more dignified. Under the guidance of Tom Kelly, a BBC journalist who became the director of communications in the Northern Ireland office, opinion polls were commissioned from McCann Erickson, an advertising agency. If the results favoured the Agreement, they were to be given to the press. If not, they should be withheld. According to a leaked government document, it was "important to ensure that not all of the results of opinion polling etc. will be in the public domain."[12]

A copy of the Agreement was sent to every household. It looked like a holiday brochure. A young couple with two children, a girl and a boy, gazed across calm seas towards a golden horizon. The Northern Ireland office chose the picture because it was eye-catching, but even idylls can be controversial. An orange sun was setting, not rising. Did this have political implications? Northern Ireland has no westerly coast to face such a sunset. The photo must have been taken somewhere else. A Belfast pictures editor traced its source. A German photographer had taken it, filming in South Africa.

After the Agreement was published, but before the referendums, the republicans and the unionists both claimed victory. This reflected the ambiguity of the document.[13] While David Trimble, the leader of the Ulster Unionists, was telling his party that it strengthened the Union, Martin McGuinness of Sinn Féin asserted at a republican rally that it was "a stepping stone to a united Ireland". To help the Catholic minority to feel that they were part of the governing process, a power-sharing executive was devised that allowed every party that won a certain number of seats at Stormont to claim a place in the government. Citizens of Northern Ireland (but not of the Republic) were given a choice of declaring themselves personally as Irish or British. Two new bodies were established for all-island-of-Ireland matters, which nationalists wanted, and all-British-Isles matters, which the unionists wanted. To make the proposals more attractive to the paramilitaries, those convicted of terrorism were released as prisoners of war.

But the war was not over. There was no peace. To win over the sceptics, Blair gave six pledges in his own handwriting, which were splashed across poster hoardings. They included his personal commitments that those who used or threatened violence would be excluded from the power-sharing executive of Northern Ireland; and that all paramilitary prisoners would be kept in jail, until their parties had given up the armed struggled. Blair insisted that there was no Plan B. There was no alternative to the Belfast Agreement. A "No" vote was made to seem like a vote against peace.

The referendums, north and south of the border, endorsed the Agreement with large majorities. The campaign was a triumph of perception management. As Mitchell left his hotel, relaxing in a job well done, he heard someone call his name.

> *I turned to see two elderly, grey-haired women walking towards me. One of them grabbed my hands and said, "We want to thank you. Not for us, our lives are nearly over, but for our grandchildren, whose lives are just beginning. Thanks to you, they'll lead lives of peace and hope, something we've never known." Then, with tears of joy streaming down their faces, they hugged me.[14]*

"Those words," he added, "will echo in my mind forever. They made it all worthwhile".

It might have been a Hollywood ending.

But the next few months were difficult. From May to October in 1998, there were 54 sectarian murders, including the car bomb that devastated the country town of Omagh, and at least 500 punishment beatings, more than in any of the previous five years.[15] In the sectarian ghettos of Belfast and Derry, the "hairy men" or "circuit judges" handed out rough justice with baseball bats and revolvers. The late Mo Mowlam, Blair's Secretary of State for Northern Ireland, called these outrages "housekeeping" and urged restraint from everyone. Meanwhile, the British government "choreographed" the Peace Process by withdrawing soldiers and releasing convicted terrorists. To show the support elsewhere, Trimble and Hume were jointly awarded the Nobel Peace Prize. They stood stiffly, side-by- side in Oslo and lit a flame for peace together.

"This is spin-doctoring in its highest and most morally elevated form," stated an editorial in *The Independent* supportively, "the managing of news and the manipulation of opinion in the cause of reconciliation".[16] As the months turned into years, and there were few other signs of reconciliation – little de-commissioning, no peace, no decline in the sectarian beatings or murders – the spinning sounded less convincing and more like the protests of a government in a state of denial. Blair's Pledges were broken daily, with no sign of an apology from the Prime Minister, who was known within republican circles as "the naïve idiot".

It would be equally naïve, of course, to expect that the centuries of mistrust would end overnight. Partly, perhaps, as a result of the Peace Process, prosperity returned to the centre of Belfast and the IRA's official cease-fire held after a fashion. But Blair's critics complained that he was turning a blind eye to the intimidation of working class districts, which led to widespread ethnic cleansing, in exchange for signs of well-being elsewhere.

The Assembly and the power-sharing executive were kept alive by the conviction that almost any provincial government would handle the affairs of Northern Ireland better than a government in Westminster. 'Consociational democracy', as political scientists call this system of government, has been described as the Western liberal's answer to ethnic cleansing, for it gives special rights to minorities and guarantees them a place in the system. But, as John O'Sullivan wrote, an expert on constitutional affairs, it undermines 'true' democracy, for it assumes that "the key unit in society… is not the individual citizen but the group one is born into… racial, ethnic or gender-based."

Nor did the mutual suspicion in the power-sharing executive make the processes of government any easier. In October 2002, officers from the newly constituted Police Service of Northern Ireland raided the offices of Sein Féin at the Stormont Parliament building, the home of the devolved Assembly, to seek evidence that a mole had been handing documents to the IRA, which might affect the security of Assembly members, police officers and the army. Three men and a woman were arrested. The police found a republican spy network, with access to the confidential exchanges between Blair, Bertie Ahern, the Irish Taoiseach, and George Bush, the President of the United States.

David Trimble, the leader of the Ulster Unionists, the largest party, walked out of the power-sharing executive, on the grounds that Sinn Féin, while verbally committed to peace was still preparing for war, and the Assembly was suspended. After nearly a year of political vacuum, new elections were held, in which the more extreme political parties, Sinn Féin and the DUP, gained electoral support at the expense of the more moderate SDLP and Ulster Unionists. After six years of the Peace Process, the province was *more* divided than it had been before it began. Its sectarian ghettos were ethnically cleansed more systematically, as the last restraints on the housekeeping of the hairy men were removed. The new Police Service of Northern Ireland had yet to prove either more representative than the RUC, or as effective, and was still not recognised by Sinn Féin.

After a further period of stalemate, the British and Irish governments announced in 2004 that Sinn Féin and the DUP were on the brink of another historic agreement, but that was not to be. The IRA agreed to decommission its weapons, but not, as the DUP insisted, to be photographed in doing so, and within a few weeks, a mass bank robbery, the largest in British history, suggested that the IRA's key units were fully operational. But even if a deal had been struck, it is hard to see how a power-sharing executive could have provided an effective government for the province. It would be like expecting the British National Party and the Socialist Workers' Party to work together in one administration – or the Sunni and the Shi'a Moslems in Iraq. They would have disputed the legitimacy of the very state that they were supposed to be governing.

This brief episode in the history of Northern Ireland illustrates the strengths and weaknesses of rule by perception management. It brought about a lull in the fighting between the IRA and the British armed forces, but not to the mayhem in the ghettos. It reconciled the British, Irish and US governments, and attracted investment from the EU, but it undermined the authority of Westminster and the rule of British law, and left the province more sharply divided along sectarian line.

In July 2005, the IRA announced an end to its armed conflict, which the British and Irish governments hailed as a "tremendous breakthrough", and prepared to withdraw soldiers from South Armagh; but, without verifiable disarmament, most unionists were unconvinced. The Assembly remained suspended and the Peace Process turned another tortuous corner to bring it back to a place, which looked very much like the spot where it had all started.[17] But on the island of Great Britain, and elsewhere in Europe, it was held to be one of the successes of Tony Blair's time in office, and held up as a model for a possible peace process in the Middle East.

As the time drew closer for Blair's departure from office, there were renewed efforts to establish the power-sharing executive in a devolved

Assembly. But there was still no agreement on policing, still too few arrests for crimes that had been committed in the name of sectarian politics, still ethnic cleansing in the ghettos, still fire-bombing of stores, which were still being compensated for terrorist attacks by the British government, because few private insurance company would take the risk; and all these aberrations were still being tolerated by the Irish and British governments to cover up the fact that there was still no agreement on the constitutional nature of the province that the power-sharing executive was supposed to be governing.

On 7 March, 2007, fresh elections were held, at which Sinn Féin and the DUP gained further ground, but on this occasion, after much pressure from the British and Irish governments, their leaders, Gerry Adams and Dr. Ian Paisley, agreed to meet and to form the new executive. It was hailed as the ultimate breakthrough, when "two worlds come together to broker a new era of hope"[18] and the crowning achievement of Tony Blair's ten years in office. It may prove to be so. That, as David Trimble once remarked after a previous breakthrough, "is for history to decide", but it is not just pessimistic to imagine a different sequence of events. The power-sharing executive may lead to a stalemate in government and become more of a stumbling block than an aid to peaceful progress.

Over the past forty years since the recent Troubles began, much has changed on the island of Ireland. Both parts are now members of the EU and have benefited from European investment. Both are more prosperous. The Roman Catholic Church has lost much of the power that it once had over the small towns and rural communities in the Republic, partly because of child abuse scandals, but also due to the declining power of the Irish 'narratives of history', as Lyotard predicted. Many factors have contributed to the relative peace in Northern Ireland other than the Peace Process itself.

The main aim of the extensive diplomatic activity that Mitchell, Blair and Aherne undertook to further the Belfast Agreement was to draw the men of violence into peaceful democratic politics. In doing so, they condoned practices that would be unthinkable elsewhere in the British Isles. They proposed win-win deals, wheeling and dealing, offered bribes, released convicted murderers, set deadlines that would be ignored, transformed the police service, apologised, made pledges, broke them, and spun, spun, spun. For some commentators,[19] all this was acceptable. The ends justified the means, but in doing so, the British government lost the confidence of the Ulster middle classes. As a result, liberal-minded unionists turned to the DUP as the party more likely to protect their interests, while nationalists turned to Sinn Féin for similar reasons. The political centre that had held the province together during the Troubles was almost destroyed; and the power-sharing executive was placed in the hands of those least likely to share a common vision for the future.

This was not the end of the matter. During the years since the Belfast Agreement, a new right-wing administration took over in Washington and the events of 9/11 transformed the Western attitude towards terrorism. The Mitchell-Clinton-Blair peace-processing in Northern Ireland now seemed to come from a distant past. Where, under George W. Bush, was the wooing of terrorists? Where was the White House welcome for Gerry Adams? Where was the *terrorist chic*, the Hollywood films that were once made about the brave rebels drawn into the IRA? Where were the funds from NORAID?

Overnight, or so it seemed, the West's general tactics in tackling terrorism switched from appeasement to revenge, from softly-softly to Shock and Awe. The aim might be similar – to protect the Free World from those who wanted to destroy it – but the way in which that strategy was implemented could scarcely be more dissimilar. The effort to lure the terrorists into a peace process was replaced by a determination to root them out of their hideaways in Afghanistan, Guatemala, Iraq or wherever they might be.

From a Western point of view, this change in policy was part of the democratic process; but for many non-Westerners, it was very puzzling. How could a government that had released on parole a white Irish Catholic terrorist, who attempted to assassinate Mrs. Thatcher and her cabinet at a Brighton hotel, subscribe to a policy of invading and bombing other countries on the pretext of rooting out other Arab and non-white terrorists, who might not even live there? How could it hold under detention those Islamic priests who denounced the Western world, when for many years it had tolerated equally fiery denunciations of the British state from Irish Catholic priests, who presided over IRA funerals and called the rebels "freedom fighters"?

There could only be one explanation: racist imperialism. And all the perception managers in the world cannot change that widely held belief in the streets of Baghdad, Nablus and Cairo, and even in the Negev desert. It is too late to do so.

Notes

1. George Mitchell: *Making Peace*, p. 11-2

2. Samuel R. Huntington: *The Clash of Civilizations*, (Simon and Shuster, 1997), p. 161

3. Marie-Thérèse Fay, Mike Morrissey and Marie Smyth: *Northern Ireland's Troubles: The Human Costs* (Pluto Press, 1999), published from a University of Ulster research programme.

4. George Mitchell: *Making Peace*, p. 25.

5. Ibid., p. 35

6. Heaney wrote: "My passport's green. No glass of ours was raised to toast the Queen."

7. George Mitchell: *Making Peace*, p. 73-4

8. *The Leader*, 6 February, 1904

9. Published in 1903.

10. Such as Ernst Renan, the influential French critic, who wrote *The Poetry of the Celtic Races*, published in 1857 and re-printed in English in 1896.

11. According to the preamble to the Agreement.

12. *The Independent*, 28 March, 1998. I am grateful to Jenny McCartney of the *Sunday Telegraph* for drawing my attention to this example of perception management.

13. Such ambiguity was a characteristic of the British style of diplomacy at this time. In *Blair's Wars* (2004), John Kampfner drew attention to the "inherent contradiction" in Resolution 1441, which was passed by the UN's Security Council. "Either military action was automatic, or it required a second resolution. It had to be one or the other." Unfortunately, it was worded in such a way that the Americans and the French gave opposite interpretations; but it was only because of its ambiguous wording that the resolution could be passed at all.

14. George Mitchell: *Making Peace*, p. 183

15. These statistics of the murders were given by the Security Minister, Adam Ingram MP, in the House of Commons and quoted by the *Belfast Telegraph*, 22 October, 1998. The statistics on punishment beatings and kneecappings were provided by Families Against Intimidation and Terror (FAIT), which stressed that this dismal record was likely to be an under-estimate, for most of the victims and their families were too frightened to go to the police.

16. *The Independent*, 11 September, 1998

17. Jenny McCartney wrote wisely and wittily about this episode in *The Sunday Telegraph*, 31 July, 2005

18. *The Independent*, 27 March, 2007.

19. Notably Steve Richards, writing in *The Independent*, 28 March, 2007.

Chapter Seven
The Perception Managers

"Did you ever stop to wonder," John W. Rendon asked an Information and Security Conference in Colorado Springs in 1996, "how the people in Kuwait City, after being held hostage for seven long and painful months, were able to get hold of hand-held American flags – and those of other countries?" He was referring to an incident at the end of the first Gulf War when the allied forces, entering Kuwait City, were greeted by hundreds of Kuwaiti citizens, waving US flags. "That was one of my jobs."[1]

He was "an information warrior and a perception manager", a spin-doctor. This was his job-description. He did not alter the facts. He enhanced the images and made sure that they were available for US prime-time TV audiences. Sometimes he chose the shots to ensure that the editors in the heat of the newsrooms, when they had other things on their mind, picked the right ones. It was not exactly cheating and, in a democracy, it was important that voters were kept informed in a positive way, which might mean some stage-management. The same might be said of other iconic moments, such as of Blair, jacket slung over shoulder, leading Albanian refugees to freedom during the Kosovan war or the toppling of Saddam's statue in Firdos Square in Baghdad by happy Iraqis after the Allies' successful invasion in 2003.

But the Boston Globe felt that there was a "self-conscious and forced quality" to these images from Iraq. When the cameras were allowed to take long shots of Firdos Square, they revealed that it was ringed by tanks and marines, who had sealed off the square before admitting a fairly small group of Iraqis to celebrate the toppling. But not every station showed the triumph of the Anglo-American forces from this less flattering perspective. Fox and Sky did not do so, the Murdoch news channels, but the BBC and Reuters did, which led on to the idea that some TV companies were more ready than others to have their editorial perceptions managed by their governments.

Spin-doctors claim that there is nothing new about perception management. In modern times, every government seeks a working relationship with the press, which may involve codes of practices, discretion and a sense of fair play. A well-spun story could be regarded as the politician's answer to a journalist's scoop. Both are ways of trying to extract the maximum benefit from the provision of news. Handing out flags pales into insignificance beside military parades, and few perception managers have the resources to match the coronations, state funerals and royal weddings of the past, which amounted to spinning on a grand scale. Nothing, in principle, has changed.

But, in practice, much has changed.[2] Governments and their advisers are more aware of the daily routines of the press, so that if a friendly journalist needs a scoop, one can be usefully provided. During the peace process in Northern Ireland, Mitchell was annoyed at the way in which some parties talked to reporters before they talked to each other, as if they wanted to set the agenda in advance. It is a common practice to release texts of political speeches before they are delivered and to seek to obtain press coverage before their opponents have had a chance to reply. Whereas once elections were fought on the street corner or at the local hustings, now they are waged as much on television, where the campaigning never ceases, and even parliamentary debates are often upstaged by the battles between politicians in the media.

Press releases are delivered with such precise timing to offices or broadcasting studios that sometimes they can be in print or on air, before the editors have had time to read them carefully. During the war in Kosovo, NATO planes killed seventy-two refugees by mistake and the BBC's Breakfast News calmly stated that the allies had "re-affirmed their commitment"[3] by bombing Belgrade, as if all that mattered about this slaughter was that NATO should not lose its will to win. This was the language of NATO press releases. The BBC journalist on the spot, Mark Laity, afterwards left the BBC, at the suggestion of Blair's Director of Communications, Alistair Campbell, to join NATO's Information Services.

The volume of news has increased. Every major newspaper or broadcasting station has its own website, on which more information can be placed, leaving the impression that it is providing a complete record of our times. Much of this material comes from second-hand sources, such as press releases, but if there is enough public interest, editors will send their best writers to the scenes of the action. But even highly paid journalists are not immune from pressure. It is a spin-doctor's duty to seek out the right ones and to offer them stories, not to try to change their views but to secure a mutual dependency. Journalists, who said the right things, might even be offered jobs as perception managers, if they wished to give up journalism. Some, such as Tom Kelly in Belfast, Mark Laity and another BBC journalist, Martin Sixsmith, accepted.

This has led to a rise in the number of what Bruce Page,[4] a journalist of the old school, called *virtual* newspapers, publications that look like newspapers, and imitate the lay-outs of the traditional press, but contain little independently reported news. They amounted, in his view, to little more than free sheets in disguise, but they were sold as newspapers and commanded a similar degree of influence. He singled out the NewsCorp stable[5] of newspapers, magazines, television and radio stations for particular censure,[6] but for many media observers, the rise of the Murdoch Empire was another historical accident that was waiting to happen.

In 1962, the Canadian philosopher, Marshall McLuhan, predicted the coming of "the global village" in which we would be linked across the world by the electronic media and conditioned by the patterns of ownership and the means of transmission in media empires.[7] By the 1990s, according to Robert McChesney,[8] nine companies dominated the world's news and entertainment market, which covered other activities, such as films, theme parks, shops and publishing, as well as broadcasting.[9]

NewsCorp was one of these firms, but, with estimated 1997 sales of US $11 billion, it was smaller than Time Warner ($24 billion), Disney ($22 billion) and Bertelsmann ($15 billion). "By any standard of democracy," commented McChesney, "such a concentration of media power is troubling, if not unacceptable", although others took a more sanguine view. These firms supplied what their customers wanted and were described even by McChesney as the "new missionaries for global capitalism". They promoted Western values. They were usually anti-racist and anti-sexist – and always pro-democracy.

But there is a drawback. In the global village, it is hard to tell the difference between actual and virtual news. In a real village, an editor may get into trouble, if a reporter spells the name wrongly of the winner of a cake competition, but who cares in a global village? During the first Gulf War, audiences for CNN had an opportunity to watch a guided missile in action. We saw it blowing up what seemed to be an air-raid shelter in Baghdad, which, according to the Allies, was an Iraqi army command post in disguise. But the Iraqis claimed that it was a genuine shelter, filled with civilians. Which one was right? It was hard to tell, for while we were pondering the question, another wagon train of disasters had trekked across our screens. Did it matter, for the shelter could not be un-bombed? Perhaps not, but this lack of knowledge might affect the trust that we place in our leaders in the future.

Through satellites, news could be transmitted around the globe with the speed of lightning. We watched the collapse of the Soviet Empire and the fires at Chernobyl more clearly and safely than those who were there. We had ringside seats. We were witnesses of world-changing events, but the images that gave us this impression were without depth, human texture or memory, 'disembedded', to use Giddens' term. They offered what might be characterised as 'horizontal' information, on one plane, fixed by time and news deadlines. The pictures were sharp and precise, 'factual', for they were happening, but they faded quickly and if the spectator tried to reach out a hand to grasp at the possible reality behind them, they vanished altogether.

In 1989, I sat with students in a cellar in Prague, the capital of what was then Czechoslovakia, whose citizens could only legally receive the terrestrial TV channels, which were censored. But one clever scholar tapped into the satellite signals that were being received in my tourist hotel next door; and we watched, on an illegal TV set, the protests in Tienanmien Square in Beijing, while these events from the other side of the world were taking place. We were sure that Mao's Republic was on the brink of collapse and that we were watching its final stages. The students were equally sure that nothing like that could happen in Prague, while the communist President, Gustav Husák, was still alive. In weeks, the Velvet Revolution had toppled Husák, while the protests were crushed in Beijing. We were wrong about both places. The clarity of the satellite pictures led us to believe that we knew more than we did, but the censorship of terrestrial channels stopped us from knowing as much as we should.

This was how news in the global village differed from that in an actual village. In a traditional village, information was transmitted through contacts and experience, over time, sometimes within narrow limits, 'vertically' rather than 'horizontally'. I grew up in a country town during the 1950s, where London seemed like a foreign country. But we knew a great deal about the local district, such as who owned which strip of land, who was related to whom, and if they went as a family to church, chapel or a Catholic place of worship. This knowledge may have been limited, but it was absorbed into the way in which we conducted our lives and into the village's feuds, loyalties and reputations. Good deeds were remembered, good lives respected, but grudges were also borne, sometimes, as in Ireland, for a very long time. In the global village we knew less about more, whereas in an actual village we knew more about less, and in both cases, far more, far less.

In the deceptive twilight of the global village, where some details are brightly lit and others deeply obscured, the spin-doctor reigns supreme. He/she stage-manages the events, directs the camera angles and edits the scripts. Governments are not the only employers of spin-doctors. They are much in demand. Sinn Féin's spin-doctors staged a road block for the benefit of the BBC's Panorama team at a location in South Armagh,[10] to demonstrate that the IRA, not the British army, was in charge. They turned the annual Orange March at Drumcree, a *church* parade, whose ageing brigade devoutly sang "The Lord Is My Shepherd" before taking a step, into large and angry confrontations with the police, the army and Catholic residents, for the benefit of the world's cameras. When the cameras went away, so did the spin-doctors and the riots.

But the flip side of not exactly cheating is not being quite believed. Jean Baudrillard wrote a book, *The Gulf War Did Not Take Place*, in which he claimed that the first Gulf War was no more than a photo call for the US army to display its might. Saddam Hossein's invasion of Kuwait gave them an excuse. This war was Reality TV, writ large.[11] But the Gulf War *did* take place. We know that it did. It only seemed less real, because there were perception managers, like Rendon, handing out US flags to Kuwaitis, which made it seem like the entry of the Allies into Paris after World War II. They may also have led the US public and even its government to believe that there would be a similar welcome for their forces in Iraq after Saddam's downfall.

The concentration of media ownership, which, according to McChesney, threatened democracy, was not only due to the fact that so large a slice of the world's news and entertainment market was concentrated in the hands of so few companies. It was also because these nine giants competed with, and therefore imitated, each other. If one bought a publishing house, another did so. If Disney developed a retail chain with a Mickey Mouse logo, Time-Warner retorted with Bugs Bunny. They fished in the same marketing pool. They each tried to maximise the commercial benefits from the minimal amount of creative input. A book would be re-cycled as a film, and then as a TV series, whose theme tune would be sold within a compilation of similar tunes or released separately, and emerge a few months later, within a TV commercial.

They had similar ways of assessing customer demand. Apart from ratings and sales figures, they relied upon market research, which made it tricky to try anything new. A new play, a new idea or a new genre has, by definition, no 'market presence'. It may be possible to concoct a market presence by observing how similar ideas have worked, or not, in the past, but this approach discouraged those who have proposals, which are original precisely because they differ from what has been tried before. The sad but cynical response to those people who come up with a new idea is familiar to all writers who have ever received a rejection slip. "Hey, folks, nothing is really new", which being translated meant, "We know the limits to the human mind. What we don't know, we can research. That is the First Law of Modernity."

Although there was a very large number of new channels and stations, it was difficult to find anything that had not been seen often before. The media giants relied upon well-known genres – quizzes, game shows, comic strips, detective stories, cops-and-robbers, Westerns and 1950s sit-coms – and from their point of view, they could hardly be blamed for doing so, for they had invested so much in digging up roads and launching satellites to install the new communications systems that they were forced to minimise their risks elsewhere. Even news coverage could be described as an inherited genre, for the seven items that filled an average newscast included a similar mixture of events, politics, human interest, sport and show business, which could have been found in most Western newspapers for over a century.

The brave new world of multi-channel broadcasting was constructed along the lines of the newspaper and magazine publishing, rather than on book publishing, with 'scheduling' replacing 'lay-outs' as the main editorial obsession. If the model had been that of book publishing, the result might have been very different. Individual dramas, films and documentary programmes would have replaced the continuous daily stream of news and entertainment. Better programmes might have been made.

The inventiveness of the media giants lay in other directions – notably in the way in which they seized on the chances offered by the new technology and brought them into being with audacious deals that dazzled investors, viewers and governments alike. The perception managers talked of an "information-rich" society, which would follow the industrial, post-industrial and services-based economies. The giants provided the infrastructure to the global market economy, so that humble fund managers, sitting at their laptops, could shift vast sums of money around the world, according to the information supplied by obscure databases, which they also provided.

Satellites were now smaller, cheaper and more widely available. Computers, which had once filled rooms, were converted into desktops, laptops and palmtops. Optical fibre cables replaced the old coaxial cables. Digital technology arrived. For the first time in broadcasting history, there was no shortage of capacity. There could be as many channels as there were names in a telephone directory. The old days of 'rationed TV'[12] and 'set-menu' channels were over, at least in theory.

During the 1990s, these giants dominated public affairs. They controlled marketing campaigns. They sold space to the agencies and owned the agencies that bought the space. They added new world federations to the noble art of boxing and transformed the even nobler art of cricket into something that was halfway between baseball and tip-and-run. They turned low-profile events into high-profile events, and, like a schoolboy who adds "The World, The Universe," to his street address, went on from there. World competitions were staged, with world cups, which came with huge prizes, but domestic competitions suffered. Party conferences were turned into rallies, without dissenting voices. Their old role as a forum for open debates, with elected delegates and the tabling of controversial motions, was unceremoniously dumped.

Political leaders were chosen largely for their television appeal. How well they performed within the parameters of a TV debate was considered essential to getting the party's message across. In *The Blair Revolution*, Mandelson and Liddle welcomed this development. It meant that their leader could speak over the heads of the Labour activists to the ordinary Labour voters. With the help of television, the leadership could construct a mass movement that curbed the power of the trade unions and restricted the influence of the largely self-appointed local party executives. It was supposed to be a step towards a wider democracy, but this never worked, as planned. It weakened the party structure through which the views of local workers could be expressed. There was less incentive to join the party and membership declined.

The same might be said for other political parties. The dependence upon television grew and the traditional structures for political activity were side tracked. In Italy, the worlds of politics and the media merged in the person of Silvio Berlusconi, the tycoon who entered politics in 1993 and rose to become the Italian Prime Minister. But there were other media tycoons, who might be called Berlusconis-by-proxy, in that they cultivated their friendships with leading politicians, as politicians did with them, to obtain commercial advantages or because they liked being at the centre of events. The career of Rupert Murdoch has been widely documented[13] over five continents, four decades and three political leaders – Reagan, Thatcher and Blair. His friendship and support for them was much reciprocated.

Just as politicians required the help of the media, so the media barons needed support in the background from the politicians. As well as the technical challenges of creating the global media empires, there were formidable political obstacles as well. Western countries had monopoly laws and there were restrictions upon the ownership of companies by foreign interests. Murdoch became a US citizen to secure Twentieth Century Fox and his purchase of The Times Newspaper Group in London required almost split-second timing. But the main threat to the media empires came not from domestic politics or taxation, but from technology itself. With the rise of the Internet and the prospect of any number of channels, there was no reason why any of these empires should exist at all. Anyone could communicate through the airwaves, a giant step for democracy. By the end of the 1990s, it was predicted that the Internet would prove to be the iceberg that sank all these news and entertainment Titanics.

In the long term, this may still happen, but in the short term, the giants sought to control the new market. They had the resources to do so. They could create the best web sites, offer the best services and could wait until the public installed broadband and found out what the whole caboodle had to offer. In January 2000 – when else? – Time-Warner and AOL (America On Line) announced the biggest corporate deal in history, which brought together the world's largest media company with the world's largest Internet service provider. They could never programme the Internet, but they could become one of the main "gatekeepers" to the global communications system. As their spin-doctors pointed out, they were helping other voices to be heard – a fresh boost for democracy and another triumph for global capitalism.

But the gatekeepers had the power to restrict or prevent access to the system, as well as to enable it. They had the market dominance to set the tariffs. They were in the best position to monitor the web-sites and the broadcasting channels. Their corporate values were the ones, which, if the system stayed in their control, would prevail. The final trick of their perception managers was to persuade so many people, wide-eyed governments among them, that their programming choices reflected the wishes of the public at large. But this was untrue. The skill of perception management was the manipulation of public opinion, not its true reflection.

The larger and more powerful the media giants became, the more they wanted to give the impression that they were really the folks-next-door. Niche markets could be left to smaller companies, like the old BBC, which was never in the top ten, but if one of these tadpoles had discovered an attractive niche market, it could be devoured and taken over like any other company. A portfolio of niche markets might become a new mass market, and so the media giants were never wholly indifferent to the tastes of enthusiasts that liked chess or madrigals. But, generally speaking, such minority interests could be left to the small web-sites or subscription services on cable, while all the media giants tried to represent themselves individually as the one-and-only, authentic 'voice of the people', as chosen by focus groups and sales figures.

They had ways of making you talk. These could be very simple. One was the phone-in; another, the listener's requests; and a third, the vox-pop, street interviews. These were easy ways of making programmes, and usually cheap, and they became the staple diet of many channels. On another level, there were game shows, chat and discussion forums, which ranged from the BBC's *Question Time* to *Jerry Springer*, before audiences, chosen to reflect a cross-section of public opinion. These were often stage-managed to give the impression that the public was holding politicians to account, but they became an effective way of campaigning, for a confident politician, such as Tony Blair, relished the starring role of seeming to be the man in charge, grappling with 'great public issues'.

Finally, there was Reality TV in its many shapes and disguises. One version was to play jokes on unsuspecting members of the public, and to film their reactions. A variation was to collect a group of people, Celebrity List B, and to place them in an extraordinary situation, such as the *Big Brother* household or deep in the jungle, to see how well they coped with the challenges. Various prizes could be offered, and the viewing public could be urged to vote for or against each individual, in what some social-scientists-cum-spin-doctors reckoned was a useful study of 'societal' skills.

By such means, the media giants confronted their critics, such as McChesney, who argued that the concentration of ownership was "troubling, if not unacceptable". On the contrary, they said, they were enabling a broader range of opinion to be heard. In their view, this was necessarily so. They were responding to public demand. If their ratings slumped, they would lose investors, advertisers and any political influence that they might have. Furthermore, by making the public so much the centre of attention in their shows, they were helping the United States to become more aware of itself – or Britain, Australia, Canada and any other country in which they were operating – and that had to be good for democracy. This openness worked on a more local level too.

But some things had to be sacrificed, of course, of course. A studio forum could not replace the forensic arguments of two lawyers at bay. A news item with 'vox pop' clips was not a substitute for investigative journalism. If you dumped eight celebrities down into the jungle, you were not likely to end up with *Uncle Vanya*. This was television, popular entertainment, and if anybody wanted more cerebral stuff, there was a time and a place for it, but not necessarily prime time on the box. If enough people had really wanted *King Oedipus* on a Saturday evening, they would have been given it, certainly, but to impose such material upon a reluctant public was nothing more than feeble do-gooding, better left to the old BBC.

These arguments were widely accepted, even in Britain, where TV companies bidding for licenses were expected to observe quality thresholds, which meant that they were expected to offer some educational content within their portfolio of events. It was generally agreed that the public would not be interested in anything too intellectual or enlightening, and that companies could not be expected to lose money on providing it, except under political duress. The class card was sometimes played. It was assumed that only those with superior educations, and therefore with superior social standing, would be interested in more intellectually demanding programmes, but they probably would not be watching television anyway.

These myths prepared the way for a grand parade of self-fulfilling prophecies. Because few people were supposed to watch highbrow programmes, fewer highbrow programmes were made and fewer watched. For programme makers, the bars that separated high- from middle- to low-brow were repositioned downwards, month by month, with giant prizes offered to those who could successfully find the lowest common denominator. At a time when there was a glut of new channels, the chances of finding audiences for new and original programmes notably declined. Most producers had to run the gauntlet of focus groups and market research before the money was released for their pilot schemes, and even if the pilots were successful, there remained the hurdle of finding suitable slots on the networks, which required more polls, more measurement systems and more flow charts.

The media giants tended to airbrush out dissenting voices from their channels, except as guests on chat shows or as shock-jocks, who were not really dissenters at all but *provocateurs*. The giants disliked negative thinking. They always thought in the active mood. When there were large differences of opinion, as over the Iraq war, these were filtered through news items, illustrated by clips, or through studio interviews and debates, where the newscaster or presenter was expected to ask the sort of questions that a person-in-the-street might ask or to hold a balance between the opposing views. This could be hard for those who held non-Western myths, or did not fit in to the system, but even for those within it, it could be difficult to develop a difficult or controversial argument in any detail or depth. They would always be likely to be interrupted, before they had reached their main points.

A strange cultural phenomenon developed, in which those who were in the best position to communicate were discouraged from having opinions and those with opinions were discouraged from communicating. It was like a big corporate stammer, for the media giants, in their efforts to seem like the 'voice of the people', were as much inhibited as those who tried, but failed, to get their alternative views across. Of course, they believed in democracy. Of course, they believed that every person should have his/her say. But it was not their job to behave like think-tanks or philosophical debating societies, for heaven's sake. They had businesses to run and while a little public debate was good for their images, too much interfered with their schedules.

This was where perception management differed in principle from rhetoric, the ancient art of persuasion. Rhetoric was a social art. Its primary aim was to raise the standards of debate, so that better decisions could be taken within a public forum. Perception management works in the opposite direction. It starts from an assumption that the decisions have been taken, which then had to be sold to the general public.

Rhetoric can be described as the art form that enables democracies to function. The final appeal of the classical orator was always to 'Reason', but perception managers sought the trigger mechanisms that, as elsewhere in the animal kingdom, were thought to be more powerful than the intellect. In the classical past, fear, lust, greed and sloth were denounced as moral weaknesses, but for the perception managers, they had a more positive side. They could be excellent marketing tools, and many successful campaigns had less to do with the product than with stimulating the feel-good factor among mentally lazy animals.

When the myths of the media giants were projected on to the screens of the global news and entertainment networks, the results could be alarming. A mid-Atlantic family with two children, two cars and a dog became the norm for human behaviour. Anything less was under-developed, anything more was snobbish. Of course, the media giants were colour-blind. Of course, they respected all religions and creeds, because they believed that all these cultural differences could be subsumed within one total brand of civilization, which they called liberal democracy.

But in pursuing these often admirable goals, they ignored the many different ways in which people have learnt to live together. They overlooked the inflections of crowded societies and the traditional devices for settling disputes peacefully. They crushed originality and creative thought; and spread the opinion that, in the words of George Mitchell, "the aspirations of people the world over are the same." They blotted out whole galaxies of stars, when they painted the clouds with sunshine.

Notes

1. 29 February, 1996. See S. Rampton and J. Stauber: *Weapons of Mass Deception,* p.5 (2003).
2. Many books have been written on this subject, among them, Bernard Ingham: *Kill The Messenger* (Harper Collins, 1991) and *Wages of Spin* (John Murray, 2003), and Nicholas Jones: *Sultans of Spin* (Gollancz, 1999).
3. 9 April, 1999.
4. Bruce Page is an Australian journalist, a former member of the *Sunday Times* "Insight" team, a former editor of the *New Statesman* and author of *The Murdoch Archipelago* (2003).
5. It would be helpful, but beyond the scope of this book, to list the extent of the NewsCorp's media interests, but several useful books have been written on this subject, including Neil Choneweth: *Virtual Murdoch: Reality Wars on the Information Highway* (Secker and Warburg, 2001), Paul Chadwick: *Media Mates: Carving Up Australia's Media* (Macmillan, 1989), and (as cited) *The Murdoch Archipelago.*
6. Notably in *The Murdoch Archipelago* (Simon and Shuster UK, 2003).
7. In *The Gutenberg Galaxy* (1962).
8. Robert McChesney is a professor at the Institute of Communications Research at the University of Illinois.
9. The nine companies were Time Warner, Disney, Bertelsmann, Viacom, NewsCorp, TCI, General Electric, Sony and Seagram. These companies are followed by about 50 other companies, which have holdings of between $1 billion and $8 billion each. The BBC ($3.5 billion) was one of these second-tier companies.
10. This programme was not screened.

11. Jean Baudrillard: *The Gulf War Did Not Take Place* (1995, Power Publications, Sydney).
12. This was the phrase used by two Home Office researchers, C.G. Veljanovski and W.D. Bishop, in the research paper, *Choice by Cable* (IEA, 1983).
13. Notably by Bruce Page in *The Murdoch Archipelago*.

Chapter Eight
The Declining Skills of Rhetoric

All governments sometimes want to shoot the messenger. Many succeed. But before we shed too many tears for the errand boy, we should consider if they are not often justified. Messengers can make mistakes. They can be in the pay of the enemy. Even if their motives are as pure as they seem – and they rarely are, not even in the case of BBC's famed impartiality – they do not have a government's responsibilities. They may cause trouble in the ranks or riots in the streets. There may be an over-riding need to starve "terrorists of the oxygen of publicity", to use Mrs. Thatcher's vivid phrase. If they have to be shot, a sensible government shoots quickly.

For their own protection, wise messengers arm themselves with evidence, such as a tattered ensign, which proves that the bad news that they are carrying is not just fantasy or opinion, but comes from a higher authority, such as a beleaguered General. But there might not be such an officer. He may have been killed in the battle. There may be little hard evidence, in which case messengers have to tell their story with as much conviction as they can muster to escape the avenging bullets. There are manuals that teach them how to proceed – how to start with a detail, which will be easily believed, and build logically towards the critical moment, when all will be revealed.

But reason and plausibility may not be enough. They may have to appeal to a sense of natural justice or to the gods, to stay the finger on the trigger and beg the powers-that-be to think again, or failing that, to hire a good lawyer, for beyond all other professions, the lawyer was a trained orator, proficient in the skills of rhetoric, the ancient art of persuasion.

In modern times, the word, 'rhetoric', has acquired an ugly ring. It has come to mean flowery language without content, *mere* rhetoric, the empty words of the salesman and the seducer, but it was the classical art form, whose skills encouraged public debates and the rule of law – and made them possible. It was the peaceful substitute for trial by combat and summary executions. It tamed the lynch mob and the mad dictator.

It was the "narrow shed" that enabled liberal democracies to thrive.

Some blame the media for the decline of rhetoric. If you are trying to squeeze a complicated idea into a five-minute slot on a chat show, you have to resort to sound bites. There is no alternative. If you are still not allowed to do so without interruption from a presenter, you must be expected to get impatient and resort to glib devices to get your points across. If you have been taught to believe that reason is a poor substitute for instinct and emotion, then rhetoric is more of a hindrance than a help. It gets in the way of perception management.

If you know that the real purpose of the programme is to entertain the public and sell advertising space for the sponsors, and has nothing to do with your arguments or beliefs, however important they may be, you are likely to feel, at best, frustrated. And this may build up into a sense of anger and mutual distrust, which is the second worst state of mind in which to discuss public affairs, the worst being luvviedom.

But the media are what their name suggests, simply a means to an end, not the end itself. If television fails to provide the conditions in which an argument can be adequately expressed and countered, the fault does not lie in the technology, but in the way in which we (through politics and trade) have chosen to structure the industry. Some skills of rhetoric adapt easily to television. Indeed, they are part of the craft of making good programmes. But rhetoric can be so powerful and dangerous in the wrong hands that most governments seek to restrict how it is being used. This may lead to censorship, but more often to rules that orators are asked to observe, which is why the laws inhibiting the art of rhetoric are almost as ancient as the art form itself.

The classical arguments that justified the keeping of orators under control and came to influence the skills of rhetoric were expressed by Plato in the two dialogues, *Gorgias* and *Theaetetus,*[1] nearly four centuries before the birth of Christ. In *Gorgias*, Plato's mentor, Socrates, met the Athenian orator, Gorgias, who sold his rhetorical skills in the market place. Clients purchased his help in lawsuits, as well as for funeral orations, weddings and similar occasions. But Socrates objected to his profession on the grounds that it was akin to lying. Gorgias was not hired to tell the truth, but to defend an interest, and so was paid to mislead. Gorgias retorted that, on the contrary, his profession helped a point of view to be more clearly expressed, so that an independent person would be in a better position to form a considered opinion.

But Socrates argued that good orators were expensive and was truth or justice something that went to the side that could afford the better lawyers? In doing so, he launched a topic for conversation for the next two thousand years or so, but Plato waited for only thirty more before writing *Theaetetus*, in which Socrates explained what he meant. Moral knowledge, he stated, was not a matter of opinion, but came from our intuitions of the ideal, which were stamped on our minds, like letters upon a wax tablet. The ideal was inherently truthful. We knew it to be so. When orators tried to change minds through Rhetoric, they merely added to the sum of human confusion.

But how were the human intuitions of the ideal to be distinguished from the moralistic gut reactions of the religious bully and the bigot? Those who believe that they are in the right, or may be convinced with every fibre of their being that they *are* right, require a degree of self-control simply to listen to the special pleading of those whom they *know* to be villains or acting in the defence of villains. But Socrates was an Athenian, whose city was dedicated to Pallas Athena, Goddess of Wisdom. He believed that personal feelings should be restrained, until, after a process of logical reasoning, the truth could be perceived, which would be intuitively acknowledged by men of good will. Gut reactions were more of a distraction than a help.

This is how rhetoric, played by Athenian rules, differed from perception management, which simply tries to manipulate public opinion. Plato's *Dialogues*, like educative plays, illustrated this process. They took place in a public square, where friends met to discuss the affairs of the day, quite unlike those temples, shrouded in mystery where the priests protected their faiths, or those boardrooms, where the men in suits cooked up their schemes and how to market them to the average punter.

The *Dialogues* usually began with a consideration of the assumptions, or premises, upon which the arguments were to be based. These were linked together in syllogisms, the basic unit of logic, so that 'if the major premise be correct, and the minor premise is equally so, then the conclusion must logically be this...' to which all would be drawn to agree. Syllogisms were the building blocks from which much larger edifices of reasoning could be constructed. Socrates distrusted orators because their flights of fancy and emotional appeals undermined the search for truth, but in his suspicions, he was observing a cultural tradition that belonged to his home city.

When Socrates was about ten years old, the dramatist, Aeschylus, whose trilogy, *The Oresteia*, marked the Athenian way of settling blood feuds, died. The story told the story of the downfall of the House of Atreus, its final phase, after the Trojan War from which the Greek leader, Agamemnon, returned home in triumph, to be killed by his wife, Clytemnestra. His son, Orestes, avenged his death by killing his mother, but this provoked the Furies, who pursued and tormented him, for matricide was considered to be worse than all other forms of killing, a denial of life itself.

To be purged of their vengeance, Orestes sought the help of Apollo, the god of oratory, to defend his cause before the goddess of wisdom, Pallas Athena, in the city dedicated to her name. She summoned up a council of citizens to help her in the judgement, and when they were divided, she cast her support in favour of Orestes. To pacify the enraged Furies, she offered them a new role within Athenian society as the 'Kindly Ones', who only tormented those who had acted without due cause, wickedly.

No play has had a greater impact upon the course of Western civilisation than *The Oresteia*. As well as being the model for all courtroom dramas, in real life as well as on stage, it celebrated the separation of the roles between the 'orator', who pleaded a cause, the 'public', who thought about the case from the perspective of their daily lives, and the 'judge', who assessed the merits of the argument within the context of received wisdom. The spirit of Pallas Athena presided publicly over the court and the search for a just solution was the common goal.

But the speaker who was skilled in the art of rhetoric could build up a case with a logic that would do credit to Socrates, so that the appeal to the emotions came at exactly the right time, with all the questions answered and the doubts resolved, and the moment had come for society to act. The ritual of the court's procedures, the open debate and the deference shown towards the judge and, beyond him, the goddess of wisdom all led towards the taking of a public decision, the origins of democracy.

But why did Pallas Athena acquit Orestes? It was because, she said, there were no blood ties between a mother and her son. Matricide was not a crime against kinship. The mother was the nurse to the father's seed. And so the myths of patriarchy were added to those of open government, a reminder that, however carefully the rules of rhetoric were observed, however democratic the process, the wisdom of a verdict depended upon the original myths. The ideal, which, according to Socrates, would be intuitively acknowledged by men of good will, could also sometimes be wrong.

The study of rhetoric was a core discipline in medieval universities and held its place in a pan-European school curriculum until the twentieth century. The authority on its skills, apart from Apollo, was the noted

Roman orator, Marcus Tullius Cicero,[2] who died in 43 BC, but whose speeches were widely studied in British grammar schools until the 1950s, when Latin ceased to be a required subject for the entrance exams to university. He summed up the skills of rhetoric, its five parts, in his essay, *De Inventione*, much thumbed by Victorian schoolboys.

The parts were 'invention', 'disposition', 'elocution', 'memory' and 'pronunciation', but these terms need explaining. Invention – "the excogitation of true things" – was the way in which the facts, or what seemed to be facts, that supported the argument and made it seem plausible, were brought to mind and considered. Disposition meant arranging the "true things" in a logical order, so that they flowed smoothly. Elocution was the choice of the right words, not just the right accent, while Memory meant the technique of selecting from a well-ordered stock of facts and anecdotes those most appropriate to the matter in hand. Pronunciation covered the skills of presentation, the body language as well as the vocal delivery, and how to behave in a manner that fully respected the spirit of occasion.

Much as we can trace the history of modern words to their Latin or Anglo-Saxon roots, so we can find in almost any modern manual on public speaking, gobbets of advice that date back to Cicero and his medieval successors. While some of their instructions may seem to be common sense, such as to speak clearly and not to make too many hand gestures, others are more specific to our Western culture, such as the respect for the Chair and to give way to questions. Rhetoric was more than just the training for the professional lawyer. It was of equal value to the priest, the essayist and the politician. It was a discipline for the mind, whose purpose was to organise facts and intuitions in a way that was easy to understand and attractive to listen to, so that the audience would eventually be persuaded and come to a collective decision.

Rhetoric came from an oral culture and the orator was expected to be speaking to a live audience, who, if educated, would be trained in its skills as well. The wary listener could detect the flaws in an argument, an opponent could muster a response and a debate conducted under its rules would be more likely to reach a wise verdict. But this kind of performance brought its own risks. The orator, who lost the attention of an audience, might try to win it back again by exaggerating – or by mumbling and being modestly minimal – until the lines of the argument became distorted. Something similar happens in modern times, when the opinion polls slide in the wrong direction. There is the temptation to seize centre-stage by bullying tactics or by trying to be too modestly charming, and the substance of the debate is forgotten, for the price that has to be paid for the decline of rhetoric is the infectious habit of missing the point.

But some speakers got into even deeper trouble, if their audiences listened to them uncritically, for they rambled on unchecked, hyping up, dumbing down, while their listeners politely took notes, without trying to test what was being said against their experience and judgement. If this flock were influential, as sometimes happened, these undisciplined flights of oratory might be converted into grandiose projects or the reverse, petty meddling, which provided a classical definition for bad government.

Cicero was a competitive lawyer, but he was also aware of where his example might lead. Like his successors, he justified the skills of rhetoric on the grounds that they improved the standards of public debate, which would lead to better government. The trust in these skills encouraged the belief that government-by-talking-shop might be practical and not a bad way to run a country. But in modern times, rhetoric has been split up into academic disciplines, such as law, philosophy and hermeneutics, and into such professions as law, journalism, marketing and perception management, which have limited goals and sophisticated ways of achieving them. It is no longer the core subject in anybody's curriculum.

Cicero's main legacy lies in the many Western replicas of the Roman forum where he eloquently spoke – the senates, assemblies and parliaments – which are as much part of our cultural heritage as churches and castles. But from one point of view, these are extraordinary anachronisms. No major company, no large organisation of any kind, would want to see its directors subjected to such an ordeal, where whole strategies could be torn apart in the rough-and-tumble of debate. Western governments often try to limit the damage by issuing statements, restricting questions, looking for speakers for support and rallying their own political tribes.

But, sometimes, the pressure of events can disrupt their plans. Speakers freeze or rise to the occasion and the skills of rhetoric come into play. And suddenly, behind all the structures of bureaucracy, we can watch the simple act of human persuasion and recognise what a supreme challenge it can be to change the minds of other human beings – and how important it is to try to do so, for this is how myths are constructed and deconstructed, so that the way ahead becomes slightly more visible.

But the British House of Commons, like the US Senate, can often seem as much of a charade as the Party Congresses of the old Soviet

Union. Token debates follow ministerial statements, in which only those committed on party lines are expected to make contributions, for or against. The speeches are worded to keep trouble away with a barrage of statistics; and the chances of converting the uncommitted are small. Where there is no attempt to persuade, the skills of rhetoric lose their purpose. They survive as flowery fragments and one-line gags, which are no better than insults. Government by consent slowly turns into management by *diktat*.

That part of Western culture which supports open debate, is replaced by preaching to the converted, or to the easily converted, which leads to another kind of government altogether, where rhetoric is unnecessary, because there is no discussion. Under those circumstances, while the government may seem to be in charge, the real differences of opinion do not go away, but lie there, half-buried and un-resolved, but keep their full power, like an arms cache in Ireland, waiting for the detonators.

Sometimes a government may shoot the messenger without thinking of the consequences and set off a chain of reaction far beyond their original intentions.

In the summer of 1985, a journalist for the *Sunday Times*, Mark Hosenball, asked the British Prime Minister, Mrs. Thatcher, a sly question at a press conference in Washington, which led to the transformation of public service broadcasting in Britain – and, some might add, its downfall. What would her views be, he asked, if she found out that a British TV company was about to transmit an interview with the IRA's Chief of Staff? Mrs. Thatcher replied that she would "condemn them utterly".

Hosenball knew, although Mrs. Thatcher did not, that the BBC was planning to transmit a documentary, *At the Edge of the Union*, in the *Real Lives* series, whose aim was to show how individuals coped with stress in their daily lives. The examples were of two councillors from Derry/Londonderry, 'Stroke City', from opposite sides of the sectarian divide in Northern Ireland – Sinn Féin's Martin McGuinness and the DUP's Gregory Campbell. In the style of the genre, the programme was not scripted and they were not cross-examined. They were asked to tell their stories in their own words, illustrated with film from the BBC archives, which was where the trouble began.

In the BBC, the programme was not thought to be controversial. It belonged within current affairs, the human interest department, not news. It was not referred up to the Director-General, who was then

Alasdair Milne, or to his deputy, Michael Checkland, as the 'producers' guidelines' required in doubtful cases. McGuiness and Campbell were the elected representatives for their constituencies. Neither had been convicted of a violent crime or any other offence. McGuinness was rumoured to have been a leading member of the Provisional IRA since 1970,[3] but his exact role was not known or, if widely conjectured, could not be proved. There was no specific reason why the BBC should not interview him and, in any case, Milne was on holiday.

But the US and the British governments were highly alert to terrorism and all its dangers. Both Mrs. Thatcher and President Reagan narrowly escaped attempts at assassination, but several of Mrs. Thatcher's parliamentary colleagues were not so lucky. Less than a year had elapsed since an IRA bomb had blown up a Brighton hotel where nearly her whole cabinet was staying. In June 1985, Shia gunman had hi-jacked a jet and threatened to kill its passengers, one by one, unless their comrades were released from prison in Israel. For over a fortnight, the pleas from the victims, the demands from the gunmen and the attempts at stalling from President Reagan were broadcast on the hour, every hour, almost everywhere.

When the immediate crisis was over, Mrs. Thatcher was invited to address the American Bar Association meeting in London, where she declared: "we must try to find ways to starve the terrorists of the oxygen of publicity on which they depend." She looked for help from the broadcasting companies, which was why, a week later, Hosenball asked his question. *The Sunday Times* was part of News International, a subsidiary of Murdoch's NewsCorps, which was conducting a campaign against the BBC, its business rival. When *The Sunday Times* appeared,[4] its headlines linked her condemnation with *At the Edge of the Union*, about which she knew nothing.

Her remarks turned a case of media gamesmanship into a constitutional crisis, for the Home Secretary, Leon Brittan, who had not seen the programme either, issued a public request to the BBC's Board of Governors, not to transmit the documentary on the grounds that it might be giving support to terrorists. Even the Board had not seen the programme. It was against its practice to do so. To comment upon a programme before transmission might cast doubt upon the judgement of the BBC's management and set an unfortunate precedent. It would place the Board in the position of being an executive, a role, which, as its appointed trustees, it was ill equipped to handle.

But on this occasion the Board was divided. Some members agreed with their chairman, Stuart Young, that they should not do so, for the BBC's independence had to be defended at all costs. Others felt that the public interest required them to intervene. The Board did eventually see the programme before transmission and insisted on some amendments. They did not want McGuinness to be seen within his family circle, which implied that he could be a good husband, and they objected to a film sequence, which showed how the RUC handled the Civil Rights March in 1968, roughly, and which was not matched by balancing scenes of IRA violence. But, when *At the Edge of the Union* was finally transmitted in October 1985, five million people saw it, including loyalists and republicans, and there were very few complaints.

This should have been a storm in a teacup, but it had consequences that spread beyond the boundaries of Broadcasting House. There was a loss of confidence within the BBC. The governors distrusted the management team, and vice versa, and both distrusted the Home Secretary. Producers wondered what managing editors expected from them and editors queried the guidelines. Milne was blamed for going away on holiday and Young, who was sick from cancer, was accused of acting weakly. When he died in August, an outsider from Fleet Street, Marmaduke Hussey, was chosen to replace him, who was best known for confronting print unions not wisely but too well. According to Woodrow Wyatt's *Diaries*, Mrs. Thatcher made the appointment herself, on Rupert Murdoch's advice.[5] It was one of Murdoch's more subtle *coups*.

There was a loss of confidence in the integrity of the BBC elsewhere. The *Financial Times*, not a Murdoch newspaper, wrote: "Independence is what the BBC is all about. It is what its reputation rests upon, at home and abroad. Where is that independence now?" The BBC's license fee was meant to protect it from commercial influences, while its Royal Charter was intended to save it from political pressure. Its opponents claimed that these checks and balances, typical of old Britain, placed the BBC in the position of being a law unto itself, but its admirers retorted that the BBC's Charter affirmed that there were values other than those of trade and politics, which was why it was the pride of Britain and the envy of the world.

"The irony," stormed Mrs. Thatcher in her memoirs, "that a Reithian rhetoric should be used to defend a moral neutrality between terrorism and the forces of law and order was quite lost" upon the BBC.[6] What was quite lost on Mrs. Thatcher was that the BBC's determination to present both points of view was not the same as moral neutrality. "Broadcasting," she concluded, "was one of a number of areas – the professions such as teaching, medicine and the law were others – in which special pleading by powerful interest groups was disguised as high-minded commitment to some greater good". Public service broadcasting in her view was a "nebulous and increasingly outdated theory".[7]

But the world is full of interest groups, some good, some bad, and politicians, including governments, are a powerful one. When Thatcher compared broadcasting to such professions as the law, she may have undermined her own case, for was justice too a commodity to be bought and sold in the market place? Judges and lawyers might make mistakes. Some might be corrupt, but their errors did not undermine the myth that there was such a thing as justice that the law was expected to uphold.

A similar argument applied to public service broadcasting (PSB). All those who had paid their license fees and were legally entitled to receive the BBC, had the right to receive a news and information service free from external pressures, and to that extent impartial. Just as lawyers may be motivated by the principle of justice, when they are defending a criminal, so BBC editors, who decided to interview a suspected terrorist, may be providing a necessary public service. An editor might make mistakes, but this did not undermine the principle that the BBC upheld.

For the BBC's supporters, *At the Edge of the Union* was an example of public service broadcasting at its best. It was not confrontational. It did not set up exchanges between two angry men for the benefit of those who liked to see a public brawl. It did not misquote or distort through cutting what its contributors had to say. It did not attack or defend the government's policy in Northern Ireland. It concentrated on the lives of those concerned, their myths and perceptions, and was meant to help the British public to understand the defiant passions that swirled around the province. Of course, McGuinness and Campbell were partisans. They might say things that would anger many people, but allowing them to speak their minds in a BBC programme was a step towards drawing them into the processes of public debate.

Indeed, it might not be an exaggeration to say that the BBC's whole approach was somewhat Athenian. If so, this was probably not a coincidence. The measured tone, the search for wisdom above the clamours of the war, the careful presentation, the lack of crude showmanship, all these were signs of the classical education which many of the BBC's producers shared. But for those who did not respect the old BBC's self-belief, it could be very irritating, particularly when what seemed to be at stake was the authority of the government and the war against IRA terrorism.

During this affair, the Home Secretary, the minister in charge of broadcasting, was careful not to challenge the BBC's constitutional status, and the BBC's Board was determined to show that it had not given way before ministerial pressure, but the damage was done. The government had been caught in an attempt at pre-publication censorship and the worthiness of the programme added to the charge of interference. But this miscalculation spurred on the government's determination to bring the BBC under a greater degree of control – and set the precedent for much further restraint.

By January, Hussey had forced Milne to resign and Checkland was appointed in his place, but soon there was a complete change of leadership. John Birt, recruited from a commercial company, LWT,[8] took over. Birt was of the Beatles generation, who was aware of the changes in technology and talked the language of management consultants. He was tactful with politicians and had a creditable record as a producer. But he was not a member of what Mrs. Thatcher deemed to be the British broadcasting establishment, and this turned out to be his main strength.

Under his leadership, the BBC's Cultural Revolution began – which got rid of the old guard of liberal intellectuals and replaced them by those of a different outlook. It was more genteel than Mao's Cultural Revolution, where professors were dismissed and made to walk the streets in dunces' caps, but in other ways, it was very similar. A new managerial class, like Mao's Red Guard, took over, with a mission to continue the purge – or renewal, what you will – indefinitely.

Notes

1. *Theaetetus* was written in c.360 BC and *Gorgias* in c.398 BC.
2. In his novel, *Imperium* (Hutchinson, 2006), Robert Harris describes Cicero's life and times, as seen through the eyes of his confidential secretary, Tiro. Commentators agreed that Harris was drawing parallels between Cicero's political career with that of Tony Blair. Like Blair (with George W. Bush), Cicero placed himself at the service of a powerful man, Pompey. He connived in Pompey's ruse to make himself master of the civilized world by hyping up the threat of piracy, terrorism at sea. Cicero, like Blair, was a master of persuasion, who lacked moral fibre and depth. It is an intriguing metaphor, but perhaps unfair to Cicero, whose oratory had more substance than Blair's and a record of success.
3. Patrick Bishop and Eamonn Mallie: *The Provisional IRA* (Heinemann, 1987).
4. 28 July, 1985.

5. The story is also told in Bruce Page: *The Murdoch Archipelago* (2003), p. 363/4
6. Margaret Thatcher: *The Downing Street Years* (Harper-Collins, 1993), p. 634
7. Ibid., p. 635.
8. London Weekend Television.

Chapter Nine
The Taming of the Beeb

The old BBC was shaped by its resolve not to become just a mouthpiece for the politicians or any other powerful interest. The wars for its licensed independence had been fought under many governments and several Directors General, since the days of John Reith, its founding father, but it was never exactly independent. It had to operate within the terms of its Royal Charter; and its license fee, paid by all who owned a television set or a radio, was fixed by the government of the day.

In the months preceding the renewal of its license, which happened at regular intervals, the BBC was usually careful not to offend the powers-that-be. In extreme circumstances, its Charter could be revoked and its license withdrawn. But the BBC could argue that the very reason for its existence was to be free from political and commercial pressures, to tell the truth without fear or favour, and to uphold a national interest, symbolised by the Crown, which was above party politics.

During the Second World War, it demonstrated this independence by being more frank about the losses and the casualty figures than the British Prime Minister, Winston Churchill, would have liked. But in doing so, it won the respect and, in some cases, the passionate loyalty of its listeners, who lived not only in Britain, but in occupied Europe, North America, and throughout the Commonwealth and Empire. For a national institution that refused to be just a propaganda machine, it nevertheless became a powerful symbol of the Free World and an embodiment of its principles.

Reith trained as an engineer and served in France during the First World War. He escaped death by what seemed to be a miracle. He came from a devout family and, with a missionary zeal, strengthened by his army experience, applied for the post of General Manager of the new British Broadcasting Company in 1922. He believed that broadcasting could become a force for good, if handled properly. With this in mind, he steered the company away from the less high-minded options of commercial radio, as in the US, and the state-controlled stations. He sought a "non-profit-distributing" status for the company, which became the British Broadcasting Corporation (BBC) in 1927, with a Royal Charter to guard its independence, a license fee and its mandate to provide "public service" broadcasting, whose characteristics he helped to define.

Reith set out the BBC's aims in programming, which were to "inform, educate and entertain" the public. He believed in the power of broadcasting to raise the levels of education, taste and knowledge across the nation, rich and poor alike. The BBC's values were filtered through his standards of propriety, which were often mocked, but still survive in an altered form in producers' guidelines. His moral vision permeated public service broadcasting, and Mrs. Thatcher was right to believe that he would not tolerate anything "scurrilous and offensive."[1]

But, in Reith's day, broadcasting was on the fringes of British cultural life. The BBC was not allowed to compete directly with the press, cinemas, theatres or the record industry. During the Second World War, the balance of power shifted. Many theatres and concert halls were closed. Paper was in short supply. Under these circumstances, the BBC started to occupy the central position within British national life that it retained for thirty years. It was the main source of news and entertainment, a forum for debates and the unacknowledged arbiter of standards in public affairs.

During the 1950s, the BBC was the kind of public institution that promising Oxbridge graduates aspired to join, if they could not get into the Foreign Office. The narrow-minded zeal that Lord Reith – "that Wuthering Height", as Winston Churchill dubbed him – brought to the BBC gave way before a broader, more tolerant approach. It drew in values and skills linked with the humanities in academic circles, such as philosophy, literature and religion. It recruited from the professions of law, publishing and the arts. It was a prime example of guardianship in a classical tradition.

Armed with this moral authority, the BBC could confront politicians and even cabinet ministers on equal terms. Occasionally it made fun of them, as in the satirical review, *TW3*,[2] the original model for many other (but less incisive) programmes. Sometimes it took them to task in interviews, where the presenter took on the role of a prosecuting counsel; or in documentaries, whose journalism carried more weight, because it came from a public body that claimed to be impartial.

Its producers could be formidably knowledgeable. A drama producer would be aware of Aristotle's *The Poetics,* and all that it implied, but also of Brecht's retort to Aristotle in *A Short Organum,*[3] and all that it implied as well. A news and features editor would know something of the skills of rhetoric. A music producer could provide a history of music, combined perhaps with a fondness for Russian orthodox chanting. Collectively, the BBC basked in a glow of public approval and the blessings of its ancestors, who, unlike the history of broadcasting, stretched back a long way.

In the 1950s, cracks started to appear in the BBC's foundations. Its TV monopoly came to an end in 1955. During the 1960s, it was threatened by pirate radio and then by other licensed stations. But still, throughout the 1970s and into the '80s, it had few rivals for the quality and range of its programming. Its World Services were more trusted than The Voice of America. During the Cold War, the BBC's voice was heard and respected, in Moscow and beyond the Urals, into the heart of Siberia.[4]

A longer-term threat came from the changes in the broadcasting landscape. In 1983, two Home Office research assistants, C.G. Veljanovski and W.D. Bishop, published a short book, *Cable by Choice.*[5] They summarized the recent developments in the field of telecommunications, such as optical fibre cable, and concluded that, with a "common carrier", including satellite and digital services, there could be as many channels as there were names in a telephone directory, an information highway.

They forecast that the public would receive a range of telecommunications services through the same delivery system. Instead of set-menu channels, where you bought through the license fee, or something similar, many programs that you did not want to see, you could subscribe to a news channel, as you might buy a newspaper, or rent a film or a documentary, as you might buy a book. A range of inter-active services could be provided – in education, health care, legal advice and shopping. City centres could be transformed, as more companies took the cost-effective and environmentally friendly step of encouraging their members of staff to work from home, connected by cable to terminals in their offices.

But who should install the infrastructure needed for the information highway? Earlier in the century, the answer would have been simple. Under Reith in the 1920s, the BBC, benefiting from its state monopoly, took less than five years to provide coverage for its services across the UK, and less than ten years to offer a world service to the Commonwealth. But this question was posed at a time when Mrs. Thatcher's government was in the midst of the privatization of British Telecom (BT), which would otherwise have been well placed to install the system. She was more concerned with breaking up a state monopoly than the future for telecommunications.

In its White Paper, *Broadcasting in the '90s*, her government made it clear that they were "keen to facilitate the development of broadband cable at a pace determined by the market".[6] But which market did they mean precisely? Their market was not the market of the programme makers, but of the large publishing companies, who were invited to bid for franchises that would allow them to run their own TV services, while installing the infrastructure for the new system.

The would-be media giants were not at all pleased to find that a state-subsidised broadcasting company, the venerable Beeb, with its high reputation and loyal audiences, was straddling the very sector of the market, home entertainment, which they wanted to make their own. The BBC was attacked as an old-fashioned anomaly that stood in the way of progress. It was accused of being inefficient, profligate and arrogant, most of all in the Murdoch-owned press. Its response was often unconvincing. They did not seem to be concerned at all that its near-monopoly status had in the past excluded not only talented programme makers, but also sections of the community, whose views were inadequately represented.

Its spokesmen pretended to see no demand for broadband.[7] It acknowledged that the world of telecommunications was about to change, but saw this primarily as a management problem. At the instigation of the government, the BBC commissioned such management consultancies as McKinsey to advise them on how to meet the challenges that lay ahead. But consultants can sometimes have almost as devastating an impact upon an old-fashioned national institution as the new technology itself.

The BBC's laid-back style was not particularly profligate, but it could be absent-minded. Producers were given much creative freedom, but as a whole, the BBC was like a ramshackle federation of little empires. When the efficiency experts arrived at Broadcasting House, they were greeted with relaxed good humour. The BBC was sure that it had nothing to hide.

Amusing anecdotes about 'the Suits' with their flow charts circulated around the BBC's Club in Langham Place. One producer related how a Suit sat in his office for three days, noting each movement, and told him at the end of the week: "It's very odd. You work hard in the studio in the afternoon, and get back to the office in the evening to do deskwork, but before lunch, you just sit on the phone, chatting to your friends!" "That is the time," said the producer, "when I am discussing the programme with my contributors!" "Can't your PA do that?" asked the Suit.

It was a good joke, one that might well have happened, but I had been through a similar process before, in another existence, and I could not help wondering how long it would be, before the Suits were telling the funny stories and the producers would be trying to laugh at them.

During the 1960s, I scraped a free-lance living by occasionally working for the BBC and Paramount Pictures. Even from this lowly position, I detected the difference in their management styles. It was hard to miss. I was the theatre correspondent for Paramount British, which was an offshoot of Paramount Pictures, but both companies were taken over by Gulf Oil, the frozen food division. Gulf brought in changes in management practices prompted by the threat to the industry from the small screen, which was roughly when 'the Suits' began to arrive.

At the same time, I submitted talks and plays to the BBC. My first producer was Douglas Cleverdon, who commissioned and produced Dylan Thomas's *Under Milk Wood*. He had a tiny office, cluttered with books, letters and marked scripts, and, if I remember correctly, he welcomed me gloomily as a young hopeful, and rose from his desk to take me to the pub. My impression was that BBC producers welcomed people like me mainly as an excuse for early refreshment.

But he had read my script. He had gone to Cambridge to see a play of mine, and in due course, the programme went out much as we both intended. At Paramount, there was a longer chain of command. We readers submitted our reports under certain category headings, such as Drama, Melodrama and Comedy, and discussed what we had seen with our superior, the scripts editor. She put forward recommendations to the next level of management, which was still not the one that took the decisions. The readers shared a desk in the open-plan typing pool – a primal ooze of filing cabinets, coffee cups and wastepaper baskets – which illustrated our status in the Paramount scheme of things, second in line for the electric typewriter but first for the Tipp-Ex.

When the Suits arrived, we were taken to a spacious boardroom on the fifth floor, festooned with potted palms to look like Hawaii, where, with the help of flow charts, they explained the facts of life to us. They provided sales figures for the year, and previous years, and years that were yet to come, broken down into regions, age groups and income levels. They were relentlessly can-do and always used the active mood, but when we trooped back down to the typing pool, we often found that we had remembered no more than some instructions to look out for ideas for disaster movies, because they had done well at the box-office last year.

This advice did not change the way in which we wrote our reports, but it did influence how we categorised them. Under the headings of Drama, Melodrama and Comedy, there were sub-groups, which could be used in combinations, and locales. *King Lear* would be listed as Drama: Family/ character part: Medieval England. If a Robin Hood movie with an actor like Burl Ives had done well the previous year, there was the chance that *King Lear* might be plucked out of the filing cabinets.

At first, the system was like a game, which we played cheerfully, because we were paid to do so, but ignored, if we wanted to rave about an exciting new prospect. But if the company's profits began to slide, or risked doing so, its rules were applied more strictly and we were given less freedom to form our own opinions. We began to feel the surge of a management philosophy that was about to sweep across the West. It came from the United States: it was as distinctive as Coca-Cola.

Robert R. Locke[8] has described "the rise of American managerialism and the American graduate business school, with its MBA pretensions". They purported to offer an academic training in business affairs that could be applied to all companies, within all cultures, everywhere. The same lecture, given to us at Paramount, could be delivered anywhere within Gulf Oil's frozen food empire. It was, as Locke concluded, "the American way of doing business."[9]

The philosophy began in the 1900s, during the hey-day of Modernity, as a way of managing shop-floor labour in factories, but was expanded to apply to corporations and universities. It broke down business management into three main tasks – Market Research, Maximising Assets and Marketing. This meant, at Paramount, that the Suits with the flow charts belonged to the first stage, Market Research. They told us what the public wanted. We readers belonged to the next phase. We found Properties, which were developed into scripts, which were transformed into films, which, in the third phase, could be marketed to the identified audiences.

This approach was alien to the venerable Beeb. There was a lofty scepticism towards the methods of Market Research that split up humanity into tribes and target groups, as if each person within them did not have a mind of his/her own. It was patronising. It led to conformity, not creativity. It ignored the traditional skills of narrative, just as, in another field, it undermined rhetoric by perception management. It was philistine, in that what it could not recognise, it did not acknowledge.

It imposed the simplicities of High Modernity upon the complexities of art.

But not everyone was lucky enough to possess the cultivated assurance of an old BBC producer. John Birt came from a different background. He was born into a middle-class Catholic family in Liverpool and received a "highly regimented form of education, underpinned by corporal punishment"[10] from the Christian Brothers at St. Mary's College, where he took his A-levels in sciences. He went to St. Catherine's College, Oxford, from which he graduated with a third in Engineering, a "terrible mistake".[11] He was rejected for a BBC traineeship, joining Granada TV as a production assistant instead, but, after a successful period at London Weekend Television, he came to the BBC's management team with a reputation for 'managerial skills' and a well-known 'commitment to a public service role for broadcasting'.[12]

He had written articles with his friend, Peter Jay, for *The Times*, in which they blamed television journalism, for its "built-in bias against understanding". Visual images were more sensational than words or statistics, and improved the ratings, but were inherently less rational. Broadcasting should have a "mission to explain". They put their ideas into practice at London Weekend Television (LWT) with *The Frost Programme* and *Weekend World*, following a US model for news programming. They had anchormen, such as Jay and David Frost, interviews with the leading politicians and long expositions, "lexpos", as they were known in the trade, or even "flexpos".[13]

In the old BBC, such programmes as *Panorama* took a different approach. The journalists researched, scripted and filmed their stories, and confronted the politicians afterwards with questions. The reports might cause anger, such as *Maggie's Militant Tendency,*[14] but such conflicts were accepted as a necessary part of public service broadcasting. The US formula, favoured by Birt, was thought to be more sycophantic, but it was popular with politicians, who were always placed at the centre of events.

That was the trouble with the mission to explain. It was not a mission to doubt, to discover or to think independently. It assumed that there was a group of important people, whose views might differ but who held the wisdom of the age. Birt tightened his control over News and Current Affairs, now a single department. He tried to model the BBC along the lines of an MBA textbook, with a chain of command and, despite the license fee, a respect for market forces. He rationalised the BBC into Production and Broadcast, with four sub-divisions beneath, News and Current Affairs, Resources, Radio and Television. He introduced 'producer choice', which turned programme-makers into 'business units', allowing them to choose where to buy and sell their services in or outside the BBC. A producer could not phone up the BBC's library without having a charge code number, because each unit had to make a profit. The casual swapping of ideas, characteristic of the old BBC, was replaced by a paper trail of memos and e-mails to prove productivity.

The BBC became a breeding ground for pollsters, demographic surveys and focus groups. One stated that the BBC's audience consisted of one hundred tribes, exactly. "Why not devote a day to the celebration of Englishness," asked a producer at a Programme Development Group,[15] having discussed Englishness, Scottish-ness and Welsh-ness, in a long catalogue of ethnic identities in the British Isles. "Why not," suggested another, "a new factual soap, a sort of son of *The Village*?"

One presenter of an arts programme for the World Services referred to the author, Evelyn Waugh, as a woman, which went out over three time zones before the mistake was corrected. Another was instructed by his producer to ask such questions as "Is Chekhov alive? If not, what is his relevance today?" There was a very long list of similar remarks that would have curled the toes of an old BBC producer in sheer embarrassment. There was a widely held opinion that the BBC was being "dumbed down". There were even conferences on the subject. Although some presenters still took politicians belligerently to task, and programmes were still being made that would have done credit to the corporation in any phase of its existence, the moral authority that the BBC once possessed was in a steep and probably terminal decline.

But the head offices at the BBC's Broadcasting House were refurbished and an exhibition centre was opened on the ground floor, The BBC Experience, which was about as popular as The New Millennium Experience. Mrs. Thatcher, who rarely watched TV herself, but heard about it through the Viewers and Listeners Association, conceded that the BBC under Birt "represented an improvement in every respect".[16]

The new BBC was constructed to reflect the demography of Britain – more regional voices, more black journalists and more Catholic producers in Ulster – rather than waves of talented graduates from the older universities. It was not more democratic than the old BBC, for it was still licensed by the government, and heavy-handedly managed, but it gave the impression of reflecting a wider range of age, sexes and ethnic groups. It had something in common with the midnight images from the Dome, more types of faces, but all smiling and singing from the same song sheet.

In 1996, the BBC's Charter was renewed with more funding, a prospect that once seemed remote, but it was another BBC. Birt tried to turn the venerable Beeb into a clone of the media giants, with a mission statement to become "the world's most trusted and respected broadcaster". But the strength of the old BBC had been in its difference from other broadcasting companies, its independence and vision, which came from its grounding in the old humanities, among them the study of rhetoric.

In *The Collapse of the American Management Mystique*, Robert R. Locke took the MBA programmes to task for trying to impose the same management system on many kinds of companies. He warned of the dangers of imposing these theories upon a management culture that held other beliefs. The BBC was a case in point. After its cultural revolution, it became timid where it had been assured, populist where it had been selective, sycophantic where it had been bold, and ignorant of the culture that it purported to represent. It was also much easier for a British government to bully.

In his book, *Inside Story,* [17] Greg Dyke, the BBC's former Director General, has described how Blair's Director of Policy and Communications, Alastair Campbell, lost his temper with the BBC. It was, according to Dyke, an "unprecedented attack on the BBC's journalism from the man in charge of all the government's information services, a civil servant of unprecedented powers." It came in the wake of the invasion of Iraq, when it was slowly being realised, but still not fully recognised, that Blair had taken the country to war on what was politely called a "flawed prospectus".

It was very flawed. There were no weapons of mass destruction, no ballistic weapons to deliver them to a foreign country, certainly not to the United Kingdom and definitely not within "forty five minutes", which was part of the original claim. To support its case for invasion, the government published a "dossier" incriminating Saddam Hossein's regime, which partly came from an out-of-date PhD Thesis, borrowed without permission from its author, Ibrahim al-Matishi, and edited to sound more threatening. It became known as the "dodgy dossier".

On 15 June, 2003, Campbell was summoned before the Foreign Affairs Select Committee of the House of Commons. In his evidence, Campbell apologised for the "dodgy dossier", but insisted that the government was defending its actions against sections of the media, notably the BBC, which was running an anti-war campaign. He claimed that one of the BBC's correspondents, Andrew Gilligan, had deliberately lied. This led to a chain of circumstances in which Dyke resigned, together with the Chairman of the Board of Governors, Gavyn Davies, another revolution at the BBC, the death of Dr. David Kelly, a government-employed weapons expert, a bitter row and an expensive public inquiry, which, to most people's surprise, exonerated the government and laid the blame upon Gilligan. The press called it a whitewash.

And yet the cause could scarcely have been more trivial, even slighter than the *Real Lives* affair that so incensed Mrs. Thatcher. Apart from anything else, it was so un-British, so unlike the way in which the BBC and the government were expected to behave. There was a touch of the tabloids about Andrew Gilligan's remarks, delivered off-the-cuff on the BBC's *Today* programme in the early morning slot that the government had "sexed up" an intelligence report to support the case for invading Iraq. Serious charges should be made in a more considered way.

But he said nothing to justify the response of Campbell, who strode into the studios of a rival company, Channel 4, and interrupted a live newscast, and accused the BBC of spreading lies, in a bullying tone, with a stabbing finger, like a fascist officer. The drift of Gilligan's report turned out to be accurate, even prescient.

Surrounding this display of virtue and bad temper stood the silent witnesses and victims. They included the family of Dr. David Kelly, the source for Gilligan's story, who committed suicide. The families of the soldiers, sent to fight in Iraq on a false prospectus, were also present, and so were the Iraqis, dead or alive, and most of the Arab world. What was at stake was not just the career of Gilligan or even the future of the BBC, but the way in which such issues were openly discussed in a liberal democracy. It was a poor advertisement for the system to watch the debates in the House of Commons or the sessions at the United Nations, where the US Secretary of State, Colin Powell, did his best to defend the indefensible, and to observe how disdainfully the leaders of the Free World treated the democratic practices that they were urging others to follow. With Gilligan, the British government took the lead in shooting the messenger, unaware of all the other messengers queuing up behind.

Nor did government-by-talking-shop seem very efficient. British MPs found it difficult to ask the most obvious questions or to receive the most basic answers. It was partly a question of time. The government allotted 7 parliamentary hours to the debate on the decision to invade Iraq – and 700 hours on a bill to ban fox-hunting.[18] It took several months before the MPs found out that the government's claim that the WMD could be launched within forty-five minutes only applied to battlefield weapons, not to inter-continental missiles, and that even Blair did not understand the difference. Apart from their dodgy dossiers and misleading statements, Western diplomats were skilful at drafting deliberately ambiguous resolutions, which could be accepted all round. One example was the UN Security Council's Resolution 1441,[19] which stated: "The Council has repeatedly warned Iraq that it will face serious consequences as a result of its repeated violations of its obligations", which meant "invasion" to some members of the Security Council and "no invasion" to others.

According to one of Blair's biographers, John Kampfner, "Blair was proud of his diplomats' creative ambiguity."[20] He used this tactic before in the Belfast Agreement where both sides signed up to an ambiguous resolution, which they interpreted differently. In both cases, it led to short-term diplomatic victories, but it was a recipe for long-term disagreements and accusations of bad faith. These were exactly the kind of misunderstandings that rhetoric was meant to avoid, and it is hard to believe that there would not have been a more incisive public debate about the invasion of Iraq, and many other matters, if more people had studied Cicero – and if the BBC had been allowed to behave more like its old self.

But governments, politicians and their spokespersons also deserve sympathy. Television had evolved in such a way that prevented the orator from being in charge of his means of expression. This made it difficult for them to present their arguments. Campbell's rage seemed Oedipal in its irrationality, rebelling against the flawed wisdom of the venerable Beeb. Or it may have been partly directed against him, for he was often thought to be the supreme manipulator of the media, the spin-doctor in chief.[21] He was an expert in not exactly cheating. He relied upon other people to put forward the government's arguments, based upon stories that he had chosen or edited for them. When this failed, he strode into battle himself.

He was quick with the sound bite, the photo-call and the scoop that might lead to the favourable headline. He was adept at damage-limitation, the retort and the blow beneath the belt. He was good for a fight. He stayed at Blair's side like a bouncer at a nightclub, a media heavy. But when it came to arguing the case for war, he was impotent. The man-made circumstances that governed the making and screening of programmes prevented him from doing so. But if Campbell felt so frustrated, what about other people, who had causes in which they passionately believed and lacked his authority to influence opinion? They could not barge directly into a news studio.

What has enabled the myths of 'free speech' and the free press to take root in the West has not been an institutional formula, but an aesthetic form, rhetoric. Its guidelines assisted arguments to be developed, different voices to be heard and public decisions to be reached. In Britain, the BBC was once the semi-independent orator, an ombudsman, one of those checks-and-balances that, according to Reith's classical logic, were meant to keep tyranny in check. It was the guardian of rhetoric. But a licensed Messenger, protected by its Royal Charter, was an anachronism in the world of High Modernity. If it could not be abolished, it had to be neutered and tamed.

Even that was a messy business.

Notes

1. Ibid., p. 634.
2. *That Was The Week That Was*.
3. I am thinking in particular of Martin Esslin.
4. In 1984, I went to Novosibirsk and presented two BBC programmes from Moscow and Siberia; and I was surprised and impressed by the respect shown to the BBC.
5. *Cable by Choice* (I.E.A., 1983).
6. The Conservative's White Paper, *Broadcasting in the 1990s* (HMSO, 1988). I wrote about this paper in *The Muddled Mind of Mr. Hurd* (published in *Contemporary Review*, March, 1989, and elsewhere).
7. I am thinking in particular of the late Brian Wenham.
8. Robert H. Locke: *The Collapse of the American Management Mystique* (OUP, 1996) p. 29. Locke is a Professor of History at the University of Hawaii at Manoa and a Visiting Professor in the Department of Economics at the University of Reading. His area of special interest is the history of management.
9. Ibid., p. 29
10. John Birt's words, quoted by Chris Horrie and Steve Clarke: *Fuzzy Monsters* (1994), p. 86.
11. John Birt: *The Harder Path,* p. 70.
12. According to George Walden, formerly a Conservative MP and a supporter of Mrs. Thatcher, writing in the *Evening Standard*, 24 April, 1999.
13. Lexpos= "long expositions" and flexpos = "fucking long expositions".
14. This compared the far right of the Conservative Party with the far left of the Labour Party.
15. Held on 10 July, 1997.

16. Margaret Thatcher: *The Downing Street Years*, p. 637.
17. Published by HarperCollins Publishers (2004), p. 270 *inter alia.*
18. According to the satirical magazine, *Private Eye.*
19. Passed unanimously on 8 November, 2002.
20. John Kampfner: *Blair's Wars* (The Free Press, 2003), p. 219.
21. See Nicholas Jones: *Sultans of Spin* (Gollancz, 1999).

Chapter Ten
The Shaping of Experience

It would be churlish not to admire the new city furniture for the arts, re-furbished theatres and concert halls, concrete-and-glass arts centres, the British Library and the Barbican Arts Centre, which reflected the achievements of British cultural politicians at the turn of the Millennium. The spur was partly Europe. London wanted to emulate Paris and 'les Grand Projets de M. Mitterrand', and to be the capital city of the other capital cities, a powerhouse for the new EU. The South Bank of the Thames that had been for so long a seedy reflection of the North was completely transformed, with new theatres, art galleries, museums and the Millennium walkway.

London was not the only city to benefit from the increased public spending. In Salford, Liverpool, Newcastle, Glasgow, Cardiff, Belfast and other cities, there were similar schemes, which helped to restore a sense of civic pride to the once-thriving commercial and industrial centres that had lost their old sources of wealth. Former coal-mining villages were landscaped and their pitheads turned into folk museums. In other parts of Britain, many smaller-scale arts projects were launched, whose aims were to promote tourism, revive local crafts and project a sense of local identity.

All this was encouraging, proof that the manifestos of the 1990s had not been written in vain. As a genre, the new arts centres were an attractive group, with bright foyers and cafés. Their bookshops were a cut above the normal sales points for printed materials, such as newsagents, without aspiring to be bookshops in an old-fashioned sense of the word, meaning places where you can buy books. It was more pleasant to visit such places than to go to an old town hall, where rows of un-raked seating confronted a proscenium arch stage with velveteen curtains at the very far end.

At the same time, many people, even in the act of easing themselves into the civic upholstery, must have asked what these places exactly were for. They might have enquired: "Why am I seeing another *Twelfth*

Night?" or something similar from a broadly based repertoire that was meant to be both educational and entertaining. Many arts centres on the receipt of public money seemed to become, in the words of Alfred Doolittle,[1] 'victims of middle-class morality', although, if they were lucky, they might have a little bit on the side in the shape of a studio theatre.

The pattern was similar throughout Europe. To prove that the state, which paid the piper, did not call the tunes, artists often stirred up as much trouble as they dared in the studios, while offering classical repertoires on the larger stages. In the West, it was a way of affirming the myth of free speech. It demonstrated that a Modernist society could embrace all shades of opinion within licensed play-areas. It was a kind of schizophrenia, 'heritage' on one side and 'unbridled license' on the other, where the young Turks were allowed to fuck, fart and defecate on public money; and generally to shock the bourgeoisie, who wondered what the world was coming to?

But were these the places to "catch the conscience o' the king" or find solace during a dark night of the soul? Would a person raw from a divorce turn to them to find a balm for bitterness? "The function of art" according to Lev Dodin, "[is] to reflect society's pain [and deal] with uncomfortable and painful truths."[2] What, here?

The arts centres could be very well run or, at least, well managed. They had marketing departments, educational programmes and fostered their links with the community, as if they were running for office. During the 1970s, they often budgeted for 'containable deficits', which meant that they made predictable losses at the end of the year in order to support their requests for more money in the following year. When this habit was rumbled, the tactics changed. It was generally agreed among the arts lobbyists that the arts had been 'under-resourced' for years and the time had come for 'stabilization grants', which would prevent them from going into the red in the future. Since so much public money had already been invested, more and even larger grants to prevent further losses seemed a sensible alternative, particularly to support the Centres of Excellence, as the national theatres were now known.

Monetarists grumbled that all this was an illusion. It was a mistake to believe that more state funding would stabilise the economy of the arts. Indeed, it might make their financial predicaments even more precarious. More state subsidy would be at the expense of private investment. If grants were used to keep down ticket prices, the state theatres would undercut the private theatres and thus discourage the angels. It was the quickest way to destroy "the trade in cultural goods". London's West End had been built in the late nineteenth century with private funding. What was so special about the arts nowadays that they required these life-saving injections of the taxpayers' money?

This was convincing – up to a point. While some Victorian businessmen were ready to invest in the entertainments industry that burgeoned in the 1870s, there were others, such as the poet and critic, Matthew Arnold, who felt that this was not good enough. They recognised that, while the box office might support popular shows, it might not be stable enough as a source of income to provide for other kinds of theatre which, though unprofitable, were undoubtedly valuable. The poor might be able to afford to buy penny dreadfuls at the street corner, but they also needed cheap lending libraries. The same argument applied to the performing arts.

In 1879, Arnold saw the Comédie Française, the French national theatre, on tour in Britain and called for a similar company in London, where the great plays of the past could be played to the highest standards and offered to the public at prices kept low by state subsidy. He wrote an article, "The French Play in London", at a time when British commercial theatre was enjoying an unprecedented boom. Unlike many critics on the continent, who despised popular theatres, Arnold respected them, but feared that they were 'provincial', in that they were out of touch with the mainstream of European thought, from Aeschylus to Hugo, Shakespeare to Schiller. He wanted to construct a kind of pan-European Memory Theatre, a pantheon of Great Minds, which could look down upon the present state of affairs and offer good advice.

British audiences, he argued loftily, were largely composed of Philistines, Barbarians and the Populace. The Philistines were the businessmen, who only bothered about what was legal and profitable, not what was spiritually valuable. The Barbarians were young bloods that liked sport and fast women, while the Populace, "raw and half-developed", were the lower classes, emerging from centuries of "poverty and squalor". Arnold wanted to spread the civilizing influence of the arts, "sweetness and light", amongst them all.

He ended his essay with a clarion call: "The theatre is irresistible! Organise the theatre!" and his words were freely quoted some seventy years later, when, in the 1960s, not one but two British national theatres came into being. By then, much else had changed. The commercial theatre was on its knees, suffering from triple blows of wartime bombing, unfair competition from the BBC and an equally unfair Entertainments

Tax, levied on all forms of popular entertainment from 1917 to 1958. To claim exemption, some companies registered as Charities, under a statute, dating from the reign of Queen Elizabeth I, for the "relief and education of the poor". The Public Service Principle hung like a cloud over what was once a flourishing trade.

Instead of exercising a civilizing influence on the market, the nationals and the regional repertory theatres were now expected to lead a revival of British theatre itself. Instead of just spreading sweetness and light to the *hoi polloi* through Shakespearian and European classical drama, they were expected to stage new plays as well, from the witty romantic comedies that once graced the West End to left-wing problem plays and the avant-garde. Slowly, the features of the large-scale Modernist arts institutions became visible, cultural supermarkets, ones that embraced almost every genre and shade of opinion, if they were "good of their kind".

But the good can be the enemy of the best. Arnold was also an educationalist, an inspector of schools, and the policies that developed under his influence brought the Eng. Lit. syllabus alive (or nearly so) on the stage. Productions of Shakespeare and other European classical writers could be seen around the country in competent productions and comfortable surroundings. While the stage can never be a giant Ouija board, through which modern audiences can hear the voices of the past, the merit of classical repertoire is that it encourages actors and directors to grapple with what former writers might have meant and to escape from the parochialism of today.

These cultural initiatives were also adept at spotting the gaps in the curriculum, such as ethnic art forms, and at allowing the young and the not-so-young to express themselves freely in soundproof black boxes. But they usually encouraged the interpretative artist at the expense of the creator, for an actor or a trained musician was expected to perform in a variety of styles and to be able, in the case of a director or conductor, to assemble a programme of many different genres.

This approach was less helpful in supporting that process of open discovery that distinguished Lev Dodin's Maly Theatre. It placed contemporary composers and playwrights into small seasons and venues, where the public could be given warning in advance. It confirmed the prevailing orthodoxies and spread them around the country. It adopted a tutorial style in promoting these art forms and often it simply marketed an old-fashioned notion of culture to complacent audiences, who were not prepared to think for themselves and despised those who did. It encouraged people to think of culture as a leisure activity and led them to believe that, if they had been to a Shakespeare play, a pantomime and a jazz gig during the course of a year, they had taken part in the cultural life of the country.

This might still be better than nothing, but the culture of Britain, like the culture of any other country, is so vastly greater than anything that takes place under the name of culture in its arts centres that it is hard to think of them as anything more as marginal, very marginal. The BBC often claimed that it sponsored more arts events than the Arts Councils of England, Scotland, Wales and Northern Ireland put together. Advertising influenced more people's choices, architecture more life styles, politics more commitments, education more beliefs, all of which, from a distance, can be seen to contribute to British culture. What was offered as 'culture' through the Department of Culture, Media and Sport was not only a fraction of the whole, but almost a distraction from other cultural forces that shaped the spirit of the times, the *zeitgeist*.

Nor is it ever possible to devise a system for the country, any country, which takes into account the needs of those artists who start from scratch, with a blank canvas or a white sheet of paper. A three-way act of faith binds the artist, the producer and the public. It has to be called an act of faith, because no tangible goods or services are exchanged for known market demands. The trade is in intangible values or myths, but through this spiritual commerce, ideas are exchanged, opinions are transformed, minds are opened and civilizations peacefully evolve, which is why even the most gushing and sentimental arts manifestos, those from the old Liberal Party included, were not entirely wrong.

But this is a "process", according to Dodin, that "you can't touch with your fingers and if it can't be touched, it can't be subsidised."[3] If a producer promotes the work of an artist, not because he/she believes in it, but because it is an easy way to obtain grant funding, this faith is damaged. If people are led to believe that they can expect to receive works of art at prices reduced by subsidy, or free, they may disparage the processes of thought that lie behind these cut-price offers.

One problem with High Modernity is that when governments come under its spell, they seek a world that they "can and must control". But many artists are looking in precisely the opposite direction, towards the world that they cannot, and will not, control. This may come in the form of private feelings and emotions, or in the spirit of wonderment that the German philosopher, Immanuel Kant, called the Sublime. It may come, as the ancient Greeks believed, as a revelation. Even with classical repertoire, we can discover what a dangerous and disruptive place heritage can be.

When artists follow their intuitions of reality, they modify the myths that shape our daily lives, even the way in which we remember the past. Our visions for the future, like our memories of the past, are constructed by our myths. We look for the signs of reality that might justify our faith, but, sadly, such conclusive evidence may be very elusive. We have to put up with something less than total knowledge, just plausibility and art, for our minds cannot help but be shaped by our myths.

The artistry lies in the shaping.

Memory was Cicero's fourth part of rhetoric. It was not an innate faculty, but a way of training the mind, an acquired skill, so that the orator, who might be a lawyer, a priest or a stand-up comedian, could quickly recall a useful anecdote or a put-down phrase. The key to a good memory was form. If you placed something tidily in your mind, so that you knew where to find it again, you would be able to remember it, when the occasion arose. This rule applies as much to groups of people, as it does to individuals, for it could be said that whole societies are held together by the way in which they remember their pasts, not just by the events themselves.

The story was told of Semonides of Ceos, a Greek poet and orator, who lived in the sixth century BC and earned his living from his art. He was renowned for the sweetness of his style, which was why he was much in demand for weddings, funerals and such occasions. One day, according to legend, he was invited to a large feast to sing the praises of the host, Scopas, a rich nobleman, but he was carried away by his own eloquence and added a heroic passage about the feats of Castor and Pollux, the sons of Zeus. Scopas was not pleased. When he came to pay Semonides his agreed fee, he withheld half of it, on the grounds that the poet had spent as much time on praising the gods as he had in celebrating him.

During the meal, servants came to say that two young men were at the door and were asking to see Semonides. The poet went outside, but could not find them. They had completely disappeared. At that moment, there was an earthquake. The roof of the banqueting hall fell in, crushing Scopas and his guests beneath mountains of rubble. Semonides alone was spared and when the civic authorities came along to find out what had happened, he was able to give them a complete list of the assembly, hundreds of people. When asked how he could remember them all, he said that he could visualise in his mind's eye the inside of the hall, and how the tables were laid out in rows. He was then able to picture who was sitting at those tables. The form of the banquet itself was the key to his exceptional powers of recall.

In *The Art of Memory*,[4] Frances Yates described the amazing feats of memory that some classical and medieval orators achieved, and the lengths to which they went to acquire that skill. One method was to create a Memory Theatre, which was often a mental picture of a large mansion with a courtyard and seven staircases. Each staircase had seven floors. Each floor had seven rooms. In each room, there were seven Places, where the objects to be remembered were carefully put. The word, topic, derives from the Greek *topikós*, which meant a place. By picturing the house in the mind's eye, the objects themselves could be recalled.

The stairs, floors, rooms and places were usually themed. Such objects as the sun, kingship, the lion (king of beasts) and the eagle (king of birds) were situated on the golden staircase, which was male. The moon on the silver staircase was female. It did not matter whether the connecting links were sensible or silly, if they helped to pick out the right topics at the right time; but if the links seemed too arbitrary, they could be more trouble than they were worth. An orator might spend as much time in looking for the connections as in finding the topics, and so the themes were often drawn from astrology, legends and popular beliefs, which provided a stock of easily remembered links and convinced listeners of the truth of what he or she was saying, because they sounded so familiar.

Students were taught how to construct a Memory Theatre, how to develop and to shape it to his or her needs. For those who wanted to dazzle with their powers, it was easy to expand such a theatre by adding partitions to the rooms, but too many places could be confusing. A Memory Theatre had to retain its shape to be useful. It was recommended that the places should be evenly lit in the mind – not too spectacular, not over-shadowed and not over-laden with emotions – so that in entering a room, an orator could identify all the topics at a glance, not just one of them. This became a principle of Western good taste. It was advisable not to leave an object for too long in the courtyard. Objects without places were easily lost or forgotten.

Professions developed their own Memory Theatres with themes that puzzled or confused the outsider, and seemed impenetrable to the amateur, which might have been the intention. So might communities and political parties. The Memory Theatre of a Republican Catholic in

Ulster is constructed in a different way from that of a Protestant Loyalist. To a Republican, the Civil Rights marches in 1969 were to protect the Catholic minority, but to a Loyalist, they were the cover for an IRA insurrection. What distinguished a Republican from a Loyalist, a far-from-thin dividing line, was the way in which he or she remembered the past, not just the past itself.

With the arrival of printing, publishing and libraries, those who could read had access to a collective memory that was vastly greater than the medieval feats of recall. This had a great many benefits, but some drawbacks as well. We did not have to train our minds to remember a topic, just as, if we depended on a pocket calculator, we could become lazy at mental arithmetic. We used a library index instead, which might be better for research, but was often clumsy in debate or in just thinking about a topic. With the Internet, we can have laptop libraries – another giant step for mankind – but we still have to be able to find what we are looking for. That is the problem.

The usefulness of a filing system lies not in its size, but in its ability to recall. A letter that has been wrongly filed, or not filed at all, is soon forgotten or lost; but to remember where we have put it, we need to know how to use the system. Instead of mental staircases, we have alphabetical or numerical ordering systems, Internet search engines and dot.com companies that do the searching for us. To make the task of recall easier, we split themes into categories, such as Fiction and Non-Fiction, Science and the Arts, Leisure and Work, and sub-divide categories, so that we know where *Biography* ends and *Biology* begins, although both begin with "B".

We invent our filing systems not to imitate real life but to tidy our minds and to help us to think more clearly. Sometimes, however, when the systems become too large, they escape from any kind of personal control. That may be when we begin to rely so much on the systems that we start to assume that they must be part of reality itself. But no system is perfect. Some books fall into the cracks between categories. Was Thomas Keneally's *Schindler's Ark* Fiction or Non-Fiction? In the UK, it was listed as one, in the US as the other. Some books are hard to categorise and may not be published, because marketing officers cannot decide on which shelf to put them.

When that happens, a Memory Theatre goes into reverse. We forget objects, because they do not fit in with our categories. That is another of its tasks. It helps us to select from the total sum of our experiences those topics that we want to keep and those that we want to throw away. We forget as we remember – to prevent the clutter that accumulates when we cannot discard what we do not want to retain. The Ulster Loyalist discards the very detail that sparkles so brightly in the Irish Republican mind.

What we want to remember and what we want to forget is at the heart of what is usually meant by heritage. We are continually constructing frameworks within which our memories can be placed and retrieved – or deliberately lost. The danger of imposing one model for a society, however virtuous and Modern, is that whole nations start to lose their group memories, their sense of priorities and shared values. The connecting links are lost between private knowledge and public order, so that even a democracy feels like an unrealistic proposition, a *virtual* democracy, in which the 'voice of the people' cannot be heard, because there is no Memory Theatre, no common voice and no sense of belonging to one nation.

The US architect, Louis Sullivan, coined the phrase, "Form Follows Function", in an essay, *Tall Office Building Artistically Considered*, published in 1896, during the hey-day of Modernity. A 'tall office building' became better known as a skyscraper, but Sullivan's maxim grew into an aesthetic principle of Modernity. It influenced the Swiss architect, Le Corbusier, and his vision of *La Ville Radieuse*, in which a city was constructed from high tower blocks, connected by overhead walkways and set in a landscaped park. It was adopted by the German-American architect, Walter Gropius, and the Bauhaus Movement, which drew together a team of artists and craftsman, including Paul Klee and Wassily Kandinsky.

For a century, it influenced town-planners and architects from the Urals to the Pacific, and the politicians, who employed them, and the consultants, who advised the politicians, and the corporations, who sometimes hired and fired the lot of them. Nor was its scope restricted to housing and offices, but spread as an aesthetic theory to other art forms, including interior design, paintings and literature. In the old Soviet Union, 'Formalism', in which function was supposed to follow form, not the other way round, was an aesthetic heresy and sometimes even a serious political offence.

But Sullivan's name was not well-known outside the United States – or the reasons for coming to his conclusion. He was much influenced by Darwin and the theory of natural selection. Sullivan commented that all animals had their essential characteristics, which belonged to their species, but adapted to their environments. So should human beings. The function of form was 'adaptation', the first law of evolution. To that extent, the phrase was coined not by him, but by the spirit of a Modern age.

In many parts of Europe, the phrase was interpreted in a socially radical way. It meant getting rid of classical or gothic ornaments that smothered public buildings. It meant trying to create a new life style, which included the latest scientific advances. Above all, it implied a political revolution, free from the class distinctions of the past. In the city squares, inspired by the prototype of the Renaissance Man, Leon Battista Alberti, each building was meant to reflect its owner's status within the society. The important families were expected to own mansions near the main square, where there might be the cathedral or the town hall. In each house, there were reception rooms, servants' quarters, bedrooms and kitchens. Alberti despised vulgar ostentation, but his architectural drawings were wholly inflected by the social assumptions of his time.

But *La Ville Radieuse* was strongly egalitarian, at least in its outward style. Le Corbusier described a house or a flat as a "machine for living". Gropius pioneered the factory building of houses. Neither of them despised the aesthetics of functionalism, quite the reverse, but they tried to face up to the practical problems of modern living, such as how to get rid of slums and urban sprawl. Their solutions were often elegant and profound. They confronted not only the grandeur of old buildings, but also the snobbery that they implied. Alberti's great families no longer survived or, if they did, their influence was much reduced. By altering the architectural forms, the Modernists were, in effect, transforming the Memory Theatres.

Many modern European cities leave an impression of a kind of schizophrenia. Their centres, inspired by classical and Renaissance models, have been preserved, but they are surrounded by districts where the old houses have been knocked down and tower blocks of low-cost housing were erected in their place. The Soviet-style blocks which spread across the whole of Eastern Europe during the Cold War might be regarded as a too bleak expression of the Modernist spirit, but elsewhere in Europe, similar buildings were raised, with flats which were once much in demand. Now they are often thought to be ugly and knocked down; or preserved as heritage sites, Memory Theatres in concrete, and, paradoxically, the triumph of form over function.

But with new materials and ambitious designs, these machines for living could be converted into shining towers of light, reflecting the park-like or urban landscapes around them, and Modernity moved on. But, in one respect, it did not. Whether in planning a housing estate or in building an office block, it sought to design on a grand scale and to suit the needs of masses of people. A small number of architectural firms competed for what were often very large contracts from governments or corporations, which was why similar skylines, dominated by artistically tall buildings, rose up in Hong Kong, Singapore, London, Sydney and New York.

To fulfil their function, architects were given a brief, which might be to provide 900 housing units and 100, 000 square metres of office space. To decide upon the size and shape of a housing unit, they had to form an opinion as to what sort of person or family would want to live in it. They anticipated that certain house rules would be required, such as "No Loud Music", no running in the corridors and the payment of maintenance fees for painting the stairwells and mowing the lawns.

The architect was placed in the position not only of designing a building, but also of guessing at a life style, perhaps to the point of deciding how many children should be reared by a typical family for one of its units. He/she had sometimes to be rather didactic – to protect the environment, limit greenhouse gases and smoking in public places. He/she had to assume that the families would not have servants or dependent relatives, not want a separate garden and not possess a grand piano.

The architect would be guided by surveys and local authority guidelines, which reflect the sum of demographic and market opinion. These regulations imposed a pattern upon social behaviour and their architectural designs had to be socially alert and politically correct, much as Alberti's designs were inflected. Nor would it be true to say that Modernity is egalitarian. Large-scale projects required capital investment and political influence. Their style might seem to be uniform, but their scale implied a deal of corporate power. This had to be channelled through a government, a financial institution or some similar body. While many benefits of civilization might be spread, the freedom of the individual to choose how to live was not among them.

To tackle such a project, an architect had to think about the past and invent a future. He/she would require a database, a modern Memory Theatre. Before deciding upon the function of a development, he/she had to consider the requirements of the people who might live there. This led on to a broader speculation about the needs of mankind. An architect has always to be a myth-maker before being a technician or be instructed by the myth-makers. He/she has to choose the *form* of living, before considering the *function* of the building. Indeed, the function of a skyscraper may not be to solve the problems of city life at all, but to promote the myths of Modernity.

The authority of many developers, like that of business consultants, lies in the convincing way in which they manage to blend factual information with speculation, so that a famous architect, like Norman Foster, can confidently assert that we should be living under geodesic domes, to protect the environment and save energy.[5] His design for the West Kowloon Cultural Development in Hong Kong, a project many times greater than the Dome, was described in its publicity material as "a model for a sustainable, socio-economic, cultural eco-system."

Such visions beckon towards a future "that we can, and must, control", but not everyone even wants to live in a climate-controlled greenhouse on reclaimed land in Hong Kong harbour, albeit one with three theatres, two concert halls, a stadium, a playground of shops, a May Day parade of offices and a small city of serviced flats, with security guards. Within these grand plans, there lie vaster myths about humanity as a species, the destiny of the planet and the nature of reality itself.

Many religions have similar visions, but few have the power and authority to convert them into plans that affect every detail of our lives, even in a Special Administrative Region of China. High Modernity has this kind of power, but it has become so assimilated and diffused into the spirit of our times, the *zeitgeist*, that we breathe it in like the smog from petrol fumes without noticing what it does to our lungs, our hearts and our inner selves.

Notes

1. In Bernard Shaw's *Pygmalion*.
2. Lev Dodin: *Journey Without End* (Tantalus Books, 2005), p.32.
3. Ibid., p. 49.
4. Published by Routledge and Kegan Paul (1966).
5. In an article for *Newsweek*, March 2005.

Chapter Eleven
Zeitgeist

In the autumn of 1997, six months after New Labour's landslide victory in the British General Election, a large poster for Microsoft could be seen on the walls of London's underground. Its colours were spring-like, a light-blue sky, fluffy-white clouds, with its icons and lettering in greens, yellows and browns. Its legend read:

Give a man a fish,
He eats for a day.
Teach a man to fish,
He eats for a lifetime.
Enlighten him further,
He opens up a chain of seafood restaurants.

There were two small images where, if this had been a computer screen, the icons might be expected to be. The first was the Windows logo, a chequered flag flapping from left to right and replicated in trails of coloured squares, signifying Start or maybe Stop. The second was a picture of someone in a wheelchair, facing a computer screen in a sunny office, with colleagues bustling around and being helpful. This blurry icon suggested: "Click here for empowerment."

This poster stays in my mind as a small illustration of its time and a foretaste of things to come. The disabled person, empowered by Microsoft, illustrated a Labour election promise: "Welfare to Work". Schools and universities were to be cabled by British Telecom, so that students could be connected through the Internet to a limitless store of databases. The spring-like colours reflected the slogan on an election poster, "New Labour, New Britain". These were the pastel shades also chosen by the BBC, the *new* Beeb, in its opening credits for Breakfast News, where young men and women (faceless, sexless) strode to work across a park into the city. The messages were upbeat. Work is youthful. Work is anxiety free. We were surrounded by posters for lifetime learning and MBA programmes. Education = empowerment. Click here.

There may have been collusion between the marketing offices of

Microsoft, New Labour and the BBC. But I doubt it. It is more likely that they were responding to the spirit of the times, the *zeitgeist* of High Modernity, but the mood could change very quickly. By March 1999, the posters had been replaced, the disabled were lobbying parliament against cuts in their grants and the new Prime Minister, Tony Blair, was promising a small army of 20,000 technicians not to cable the schools but to save the country from the Millennium Bug. As the internal clocks within the computer systems ticked over from 1999 to 2000, it was feared that all the noughts would confuse them. Our bank accounts, tax records and such measurement systems would break down in panic. The country would be brought to a standstill. But they didn't, it wasn't and we were all spared.

Zeitgeists can change slowly as well as quickly, over a generation and more. For many old Labour supporters, old Liberals, like me, or old Tories, there was something rather irritating in the way in which the Microsoft poster took an ancient proverb and added a smart-Alec punch line. "Teach a man to fish and he eats for a lifetime" has the ring of truthfulness. It is a principle that can be widely applied. But not everyone even wants to own a chain of seafood restaurants. It was a gag. Living was God's way of making money, ha-ha. Enlightenment meant becoming very rich.

Our education policies were linked with employment. There was a debate about whether schools and colleges were delivering the numeracy and literacy skills, which companies required, as if that was all that mattered. The horizon of possibilities seemed to draw closer, day-by-day, in a reverse perspective, and on every foreshortened hill towered the three most chilling words in the English language, Human Resources Management.

The punch line was intended to provoke. It was meant to amuse those who were on-message by poking fun at the ideas of those who were off it, a sign of what was still being called "Cool Britannia". If so, it could have been more sharply worded. "Enlighten him further" is a heavy paraphrase for "teach" and the gag fails to follow through the proverb's form, which is an "either/or" and not "ready/steady/go". In ballroom dancing terms, it is like mistaking a foxtrot for a waltz. The key words in the proverb were *give* and *teach*. The stress on the poster was switched to *fish* to set up "sea-food restaurants", but since the proverb was not about fishing, but about *giving* and *teaching*, the punch-line failed to connect with its target or any target, except one, its own chin. But who would even notice that the leading IT company, Microsoft, a multi-trillion dollar Internet gateway, was publicising itself by missing the point?

The abuse of the proverb rang one alarm bell. The stillness of the sky set off another. The Windows sky was in fashion that season, officially called "Clouds" in its catalogue of screen savers. The clouds always seemed to be passing, but never did so. The showers threatened, but never fell. The sun never quite shone and the birds never sang, missing the point, some might think, of spring. It was as if the publicity agency had decided that the best way to brand Microsoft Windows was to capture a moment of suspended animation, full of promise but unfulfilled, and prolong it into something spring-like, but not precisely Spring, which passes into Summer and Autumn, unlike Windows, which renewed itself only after every second or third year.

"Clouds" came up on my screen, whenever I switched on my computer, and on to the screens of millions of other Windows users, to the extent that it was difficult to look at a real sky without feeling a twitch of post-modern irony. "That's odd. The clouds are actually moving. Where do we switch them off?" For a software company, the campaign must have made good sense, for software programmes are a means to an end, a process of becoming and not the end in itself. But other PR agencies must have been looking at similar manuals, for the BBC and New Labour were being publicised in the same spring-like-but-not-exactly-spring way. They had been through difficult periods of transition, but, instead of wanting to get out of them quickly, they seemed to enjoy their growing pains, and put them on their billboards, so that almost the only thing that was known about them was that they were about to become something else.

Other ages have used, and abused, spring in a similar manner. The Victorians sold chocolates with images of lambs and daffodils. Fluffy white clouds were painted on blue baroque ceilings, before Microsoft decorated our computer screens with them. But in times gone by, spring was usually one season among four. It was a popular theme with artists, the Four Seasons, useful for contemplating the passing of time. Each season had its virtues and vices, its beautiful and ugly sides. Spring was the time for romance and young lovers, but also for jealousy and shallowly rooted affections. "Rude winds do shake the darling buds of May". Summer offered fulfilment, but came with plagues and pestilence. The ripeness of autumn turned to rottenness, while winter's austerity led to wisdom, death and growth underground. Artists once employed the changing year as a metaphor for the human condition, but not now, not just before the new Millennium. This was the time for a never-ending, virtual spring.

Perhaps it was a side effect of marketing that we got into the habit of elevating spring above the other seasons and detaching it from the rest of the year. Any firm promoting a product, any politician launching a campaign or any large organisation in the throes of change always liked to turn to spring for another plunge into the Fountain of Youth. It was the sensible thing to do. Spring was the right time of year for those who wanted to grow young gracefully. When it was only one season among four, and the other seasons were shaking their heads at it more in sorrow than anger, it was a less efficient marketing tool. But in a modern world, it was always spring, somewhere. That was one of the benefits of globalisation. You could always fly off to the Bahamas in winter or to Bali in the fall. It was just a matter of money.

Our airwaves, like our posters, were filled with spring-like sounds and images, which missed the point of spring, for there were no signs of growth, no bursting into flower, no miraculous transformation, only the promise of all these things, which we took at their face value, until we noticed the stillness of the Microsoft clouds.

When you live within a *zeitgeist*, as all of us do, it can be very hard to see it for what it is, a miasma of unquestioned assumptions and unchallenged myths. The pressures of work, loyalties, heritage and laziness create a tunnel vision, in which your eyes see what they have been directed to see and your mind only thinks what it has been taught to think. But if you step to the fringes of that mist, a range of other possibilities comes into view. From a small distance, the spirit of the times in which you may have been living, or still are, can seem strange and even slightly mad. The first challenge for the theatre critic, or any other kind of critic, is how to make the familiar seem exotic and the exotic familiar, for otherwise it would be difficult to know what to recommend.

If you take the Damian Hirst catamaran down the Thames from the old Tate Gallery, which is now known as Tate Britain, to the former Bankside Power Station, which is now called the Tate Modern, calling at the London Eye by Waterloo Station, you pass by buildings on both banks, which are like public Memory Theatres. They contain the spirits of their times, their myths and beliefs, which, although familiar, are nowadays almost completely irretrievable. But there is another spirit as well, High Modernity, expressed not only in the anonymous, high-rise, concrete-and-glass buildings that now dominate the skyline, but also in the conversions, the walkways and bridges, the offices, shops, and the reasons for their existence. From this dominant and brooding presence, it can be very difficult to escape.

The Tate Gallery represented the spirit of Victorian philanthropy, inspired by Modernity in its prime. It was built in the 1890s on the site of a foul prison, but its neo-classical pillars and portico spoke of a new age of reason. Its founder, Henry Tate, made his money from sugar cubes, which he pioneered. His was a rags-to-riches story, guided by his Unitarian faith. He believed, like Matthew Arnold, in the redemptive power of art, *sweetness and light*, and gave his collection of paintings and sculptures, mainly by British artists, to the whole nation, to be viewed by the public, free of charge. When no space could be found at the National Gallery, he commissioned and paid for the new building anonymously. In due course, but not prematurely, he was publicly honoured.

But the Tate Gallery looks nothing like the Palace of Westminster, nearby on the north bank, deliberately so, for the Tate's architect, Sydney R.J. Smith, was told to leave out the patriotic symbols in favour of a pan-European Classicism. The Palace, which contains the Houses of Parliament, was built in the 1860s and its architect, Charles Barry, was invited to match Westminster Abbey nearby, so that the new building would reflect a blending of Church and State. It was constructed on the site of the ancient palace of Edward the Confessor, long demolished, but its form was meant to recall the line of medieval rulers, from which, according to historical legend, modern British civil liberties were drawn.

A statue of Simon de Montfort, the leader of the baronial revolt against King John, stands with Oliver Cromwell, the Lord Protector of the Commonwealth, in its grounds. This palace does not celebrate a line of kings, but a story of constitutional struggle, from which British democracy arose. Now it is guarded against international terrorism by concrete walls and metal fences, a visual reminder that democracy is under threat, from outside and, some might add, from managerial politics and weak opposition within. The Memory Theatre of civil liberties is now behind bars.

Across the river is an example of 1950s Modernity, the Royal Festival Hall, polite and respectable, with a curved roof like "a baby's bottom", according to Sir Thomas Beecham. Beside it stands Sir Denys Lasdun's National Theatre, but now the Royal National Theatre, built like a nuclear bunker, Modernity during the Cold War. Continental state theatres had revolutionary origins, which is why they were called national. They represented the people, unlike the old royal or court theatres. London's National Theatre had no revolutionary origins, but, when it was first built in the 1970s, it tried to seem like a bit republican. Its posters claimed:

"The National Theatre Is Yours". But it became nervous in the 1980s that it might lose its marketing battles to the Royal Shakespeare Theatre, the other national theatre; and so it changed its name to a superior form of branding, royalty.

At the end of this short journey, stand two monumental buildings, St. Paul's Cathedral, on the north bank, and the former Bankside Power Station, built by Giles Gilbert Scott, now the Tate Modern, on the south. From the Golden Globe at the top of St. Paul's Cathedral, you can see the dimensions of London, as Christopher Wren conceived them, a vision of an Enlightenment City, with rational worship at its heart. They stretched south to Richmond and Greenwich, north to Hampstead, and although the M25 motorway now surrounds an even greater area, his grand plan is still visible, a Memory Theatre of a capital and its citizens, commemorated on their tombs with classical and Christian ornamentation, as if they were heroes from an ancient world. The cathedral, which was finally completed in 1710, embodied a late flowering of Renaissance architecture, influenced by Alberti, but merging towards the new style of the Baroque. Wren was buried in St. Paul's in 1723, the first tomb in the building, and his epitaph was in Latin: "Si monumentum requiris, circumspice".[1]

The Bankside Power Station, with its twin at Battersea, represented a different vision as to how people live together, within a giant socio-industrial complex, whose services, like power, were provided by the state. Both power stations were designed by Gilbert Scott and influenced by the Bauhaus tradition. Their forms did not merely follow function: they asserted it. They elevated function above everything else. They not only served a purpose, but excluded other purposes. The chimneys are nothing but chimneys, but designed to be elegantly tall and symmetrical, a model for chimneys. The Turbine Hall at the Bankside Power Station was meant to be just a turbine hall, which makes it even odder that it should have been transformed by the alchemy of post-Modernity into something completely different – a very large art gallery with one enormous hall for installations that could be installed almost nowhere else.

The Bankside Power Station was built in two stages, 1947 and 1963. In 1964, when the British political leader, Harold Wilson, inspired the Labour Party with talk of the "white-heat of technology" that would regenerate the nation, he might have had something like these power stations in mind. But the usefulness of the power stations turned out to be short-lived. They were meant to generate electricity by burning coal, but this caused air pollution, the London smogs, and when they were converted to oil, they became too expensive to run. The Tate Gallery bought the Bankside Power Station in 1994 as a gallery for modern art. By this time, the Tate had moved far from the vision of Henry Tate. It was a brand name, more famous for art than sugar, with two regional branches, Tate St. Ives and Tate Liverpool. Its guiding principles were now no longer sweetness and light, but concepts and art history.

The Tate Modern was scheduled to open for the new Millennium and funded as a Millennium project from the National Lottery. Unlike the Dome, it was late, but a great success. Its attendance figures were much in excess of those predicted. Nearly everything in it, including its toilet paper, found sponsors. It had a good restaurant, with views of St. Paul's. Here the spirit of High Modernity seems at its most benign, but the Tate Modern has much in common with the Dome. Its exhibition spaces have educational titles, like the Dome's zones, such as the Environment/Landscape, which cut across more traditional forms of presentation, by artist, genre or historical school. The Tate Modern celebrates public virtues rather then private ones, Humanity rather than individual human beings, and so, like the Dome, it has to be very large.

The Bankside Power Station is not the only building to have been put to post-modern purposes. In a prime site, opposite the Palace of Westminster stands the old County Hall, formal, plain and official, completed in 1933, in a style often known as Bankers' Georgian, but more correctly as Edwardian Baroque. A Japanese company bought and converted it into flats, offices, corporate reception suites, an aquarium and a Salvador Dali gallery. The Henry Tate of our times, Charles Saatchi, an advertising executive and perception manager, the patron and benefactor of BritArt, had a gallery there, bearing his name. But the building still looks like a town hall. You instinctively expect to renew a driving license there.

The new City Hall, which replaced County Hall, looks like a section of a fly's eye, much magnified, smothered in reflective surfaces. On the north bank, there is a Norman Foster office building, the Gherkin, which is currently seeking its tenants, but this does not really matter, for its tenants will come and go, but the new Gherkin is already part of the skyline. To disguise their scale, these buildings have been clad in mirrors, which reflect the sky, buildings and passers-by, but they are still very large. They dominate without being wholly visible. Their shining scales are like sunglasses, as worn by the stars. It is hard to know what is going on behind them. They disguise their intentions. They are forms that can be adapted to many functions, but only, of course, as open-plan offices, with lots of people and lifts. They can be re-cycled, from one company to another, like superior packaging.

If you peer beyond these reflective surfaces and into the mission statements of the corporations that own them, it is still rather hard to find out what these buildings are actually for. PriceWaterhouseCooper, the international management consultancy, has its London offices at Charing Cross under its own arch, so monumental that it might be mistaken for an Arc de Triomphe. The PWC website is smothered in good intentions. It says: "the reputation of PWC is anchored in the professionalism, ethics and excellence of (its) service", but "times are changing". It invites you to look at its Code of Conduct. This Code asks you to look at its Values, expressed in threes, starting with Teamwork, Excellence and Leadership. These are sub-divided into Relationships, Respect and Sharing + Innovation, Learning and Agility + Courage, Vision and Integrity. But the website stops short of telling anybody what PWC actually does. That seems to be privileged information.

PWC is a brand name, which can be applied to any management service, managing almost anything, although it began as a firm of accountants. It has much in common with other brand names, logos and mission statements that populate this part of London. The name of Damian Hirst, the leader of the already ageing BritArt brat-pack, can be attached to a catamaran, a restaurant or an ashtray. Branding belongs to the aesthetics of High Modernity. It connects traditional art forms with the 'creative industries'. A brand name is a sign of success. It endorses another product with the glamour of its name, but the logo is for sale. That is why it is successful. The endorsed product may not also be not quite what it seems, just as the OXO tower, the brand name of a beef cube, has been re-cycled into shops, offices and restaurants.

Dominating the proceedings, like an orchestral conductor on a podium, is the London Eye, the giant Ferris wheel by Waterloo Station, another Millennium project, which has turned central London into a tourist attraction. The views from its glass pods are spectacular. Unlike the Golden Globe at St. Paul's Cathedral, it looks inwards, not outwards. You can see into the churches, empty apart from the memorial services and midday concerts. You can peer into the gardens at Buckingham Palace and over the fortifications that now surround the mother of parliaments. You can gaze along the Thames in both directions over award-winning reflective surfaces and re-cycled 'heritage protection zones'; and speculate about what might be going on inside them. The vistas are spruced-up and spring-like, shining like a model village.

At the same time, you cannot help wondering what would happen to London, if its tourists stopped coming and its service industries were out-sourced to other parts of the world, where labour is cheaper and the climate better. Who would live in London then? What goods would it produce? What values would it proclaim? Would they all be smothered in good intentions and mission statements? What people would be bound to their London boroughs by loyalty? Where would that loyalty start?

In the event of an attack, who would be willing to die for it?

Nothing was quite what it seemed, but the surfaces reflected all that was there.

A peace process was something that never led to a peace agreement. The aim of information was perception management. Innocence meant washing your hands of an atrocity. Heritage was protected in designated zones, in order to be forgotten. Idealism was akin to fanaticism and belonged to the other side. In a Conran restaurant, as in other parts of the Habitat empire, an untidy napkin was a portent of chaos. There was very little difference between a mission statement and party propaganda.

Scripts were released to the media of speeches that were never delivered. An ill wind in New York signified a good day to bury bad news in London. Policies became pledges, which were re-cycled as initiatives, whose good intentions got in the way of action; but, at the same time, the actions got in the way of the intentions. New measurement systems were devised to correct the errors in the old systems, and reports were issued from influential think-tanks in time to make the breakfast news, which were forgotten by lunchtime.

Power had rarely been so centralised or so eager to seem in touch, although, if necessary, grass-root support could always be astro-turfed. No British Prime Minister other than Blair has tried to seem more Alpha-Male. "Five times a night!" his wife, Cherie, confided to a *Sun* journalist, "Are you jealous?" But he wanted to appear on top of his game, for his instincts were those of an action man. No other British government has invaded a foreign country to conduct a war, whose doubtful legality was based on a clause in a Security Council resolution that British diplomats had carefully drafted to mean different things to different people.

No other British Prime Minister would have justified the war on the basis of misleading information from the Security Services, which was made to sound more convincing by his perception managers, but which he did not fully understand and turned out to be wrong. No other Prime

Minister would have won a General Election under those circumstances, albeit with a greatly reduced majority, or gone on to justify the Iraq war retrospectively, on the grounds of the increased terrorist threats. No other Prime Minister would have defended Western values with such protestations of personal integrity, while undermining them so completely.

Few battles have seemed more shadowy or closer to hand than the war against terror. The plot was that of a Bond film, in which an evil genius, Osama Bin Laden, holed up in the mountain caves of the Hindu Kush, manipulated gangs of murderous assassins through Islamic websites and something like thought control. The sequences were those of disaster movies: hi-jacked planes, collapsing towers and foreign backpackers. The use of the word, 'terror', was pure Hollywood, a battle between good and evil, with no questions asked and no quarter given. Terror, by definition, is always something wicked, but an alliance against terror falls apart, if you cannot define what that wickedness might actually mean. It was a time to defend democracy by teaming up with tyrants. Suddenly, the world became full of virtual democracies.

It was a time for letting terrorists out of prison, if they were white and Irish, but for interning possible terrorists without trial, if they seemed to be Islamic militants – double standards all round, for it offended Moslems and Ulster's law-abiding middle-classes alike. It was a time for signing the European Convention on Human Rights, and for tabling an appropriate Bill in the Commons, which needed to be re-drafted a few years later, when human rights turned out to be more negotiable than supposed. It was a time for defending free speech by condemning extremism and for seeking the powers to deport radical Islamic clerics to friendly countries, where they stood a good chance of being tortured and executed.

"The rules have changed!" said Blair defiantly, after the suicide bombings in London in July, 2005. The citizens of London were praised for their stoicism. The spirit of the Blitz was recalled. But the British have had much experience of such attacks, particularly in Belfast, and survived with something like the rule of law intact. In this case, the government responded with a flap of initiatives, which would curb freedom of speech, habeas corpus and, for suspected terrorists, trial by jury. Without publicity, more police were armed and, under certain circumstances, a shoot-to-kill policy was approved. In one accident, a Brazilian immigrant worker with an out-of-date visa was shot eight times in the head by a misinformed marksman, and the police immediately issued a false statement that had later to be retracted.

It was a bad time to be treated like a liberal, but a good time to behave like one. There were plenty of opportunities. In the First World War, one definition of a liberal was of someone who defended the rights of conscientious objectors, without necessarily being a pacifist. For some non-liberals, this seemed to condone pacifism, which was even more unpatriotic than the straightforward refusal to fight. In the war against terror, liberals were those who defended the right of Islamic clerics to hold extreme opinions, while not holding such views themselves. While non-liberals were calling for their internment or their forceful removal to the countries of their origins, liberals defended their right of free speech, if it were not an incitement to violence.[2]

The roots of liberalism lay in the many Protestant sects that grew up during the Age of Enlightenment, whose practices might vary, but were bound together by the myth that each individual had the right to pray to God, without the intervention of priests or the state. Freedom of worship was held to be the guardian of all the other freedoms, the supreme principle, which had to be defended, even though it might mean protecting those who despised the very tolerance from which they benefited.

The Anglican churches may have been poorly attended, but the evangelical missions were doing rather well. Soul records were high in the charts. In the London underground, the posters for visiting preachers put those of Microsoft in the shade and their claims were even more extravagant, no less than the Kingdom of Heaven. But for Anglican Protestants, there were no fixed certainties, no absolutes, and the only way to discover a version of a limited truth was through thought, intuition and worship. It was a painful process and they often seem so unsure of themselves, so tentative even in their opposition to the intolerable and the unforgivable, that it required a leap of the historical imagination to remember how, in times gone by, that very uncertainty hardened into a rocklike resolution that defied the fire and the sword.

It was a bad time to be a protestant, but a good time to protest.

Notes

1. "If you require a monument, look around you."
2. The *Independent*, perhaps the most liberal of British newspapers, was the only one to give prominence to the report that there were "no links between the 7 July and 21 July [terrorist] attacks", "no evidence of a terror mastermind in Britain" and that "bombers [were] radicalised in gyms, not mosques" (13 August, 2005). Other papers either ignored this report or gave it little coverage.

Chapter Twelve
Revelation

More than any other political system, a liberal democracy relies upon common sense, a trained intuition. Other forms of government may not need it so much. There are, and always have been, benevolent theocracies, while civilizations have survived along the lines of Plato's Republic, where philosophers advise an absolute ruler, whose authority comes from the gods or an ancient lineage. Other societies have jogged along on a mixture of family loyalties and tradition, where the powers of an overlord are curbed by the need to avoid tribal feuds and to placate the ancestors.

In a democracy, however, the individual elector has to make up his/her mind on the matters of the day, and to decide which leader or political party to support. Even though his/her vote may signify one voice among millions, and may only be required at irregular intervals, it is nevertheless the supreme authority. To meet this obligation, he/she has to have access to many sources of information, many opinions, and take part in what John Milton called "the open market place of ideas".

The free press and democracy have been more or less inseparable concepts since the origins of parliamentary government in England during the seventeenth century. In the US, Freedom of the Press is a right guaranteed by the First Amendment. It is enshrined within the Universal Declaration of Human Rights, which states that this right includes the "freedom to hold opinions without interference and to seek, receive and impart information and ideas through any media regardless of frontiers." Together with the Freedoms of Speech and Worship, it is a principle that is supposed to distinguish the Free World from the not-so-Free World elsewhere.

But it is a very complicated principle, if it is a principle at all, with many exceptions. Various doctrines of free will, upon which the other freedoms depended, were present in Christianity, Judaism and Islam, but the choice was usually presented as doing either good or evil, nothing in between. The Christian debate was primarily concerned with whether

God, being all-powerful and all-knowing, determined human decisions or if He allowed people to be free, despite the fact that He knew exactly what they were going to do. Protestantism offered another side to this riddle. Were individual Christians entitled to pray directly to God without the intervention of the established Church? If you believed that God had made His will known through the Church, the answer was "No", but if the Church was thought to be 'man-made', not 'God-made', the answer was "Yes". Continental wars were fought on this issue.

Freedom of worship was the underlying myth that prompted Milton to challenge the state licensing of publishers in *Areopagitica* (1644), which attacked pre-publication state censorship whereby all printed material was issued under a government license. He argued that state licensing prevented ideas and information from being spread among the general public, and therefore prevented the individual from adequately following his/her conscience. Some fifty years later, this practice was abandoned, a notable victory for the anti-censorship lobby, which led to an extraordinary rise in all forms of publishing during the eighteenth century. But there were still laws against sedition, corruption and blasphemy; and publishers could still be prosecuted if they published anything that was thought to be irreligious or obscene.

The father of liberalism, John Locke, sought a theoretical compromise. While an individual was entitled to freedom of thought and speech, he placed some of these rights in trust with the government within a social contract, which was intended to protect his wellbeing and that of his family. But the extent to which a government was entitled to intervene became a large topic for debate. A whole library could be built to contain the books written upon this subject by such writers as Voltaire, John Stuart Mill and George Orwell, together with a long list of legal case histories. It is a contentious subject today. Is the government entitled to curb the fury of fiery Islamic preachers? Or priests in Ulster? Milton and Orwell would certainly have disapproved of the Office of Communications (OFCOM). They would fear that a government might refuse a license to a TV company that offended it, as once may have happened.[1]

But would they have approved of the alternative, the still largely unregulated free market of the Web? Perhaps, on balance, but it is still hard to believe that they would have shown much enthusiasm for it. During the Iraq war, we could receive news from bloggers[2] in Baghdad, who gave us first-hand accounts of the mayhem in the streets. These were more vivid and convincing that the ones we received through the media giants, particularly those, like Fox, who supported the invasion.

From this point of view, they were to be welcomed.

Unfortunately, some bloggers were as unreliable as the media giants and less predictable. Their methods for distributing information through their networks were arbitrary. This kind of eye-witness blogging often amounted to global gossip, which could be interesting and useful, but it might not help us to make up our minds. We do not know if the bloggers are honest or whether they are telling their stories in ways that we can understand. On the Internet, there is a continual risk of fraud, viruses and contamination, and we cannot employ that conceptual apparatus that, in our daily lives, we bring to the recognition that some narratives are more plausible than others.

When we are confronted by a phenomenon that nearly resembles free speech, our first impression must be one of sheer confusion. Whom should we trust? Whose voices do we hear? In our own non-global societies, wherever, we are used to facing a much shorter list of facts and opinions, which makes it easier to choose between them. In some democracies, the list is so short, and the items so bland and interchangeable, that the voter scarcely needs to bother about free speech. A limited vocabulary of positive and negative sounding words is enough.

But even in the most open of societies, and there are organisations[3] that can tell us which these are, a filtering system blots out much of the potential information. State censorship is only a small part of it. Our wish to get on well with our neighbours is often a more powerful force. The *zeitgeist* is stronger still. Official censorship may even sometimes be more liberal than social censorship. It may try to ban bigotry and snobbishness. It may try to promote political correctness. In the old Soviet Union, it was often believed that the state censorship from Moscow was more reliable than the arbitrary bans of local party *apparatchiks*. Within our minds, we censor. We ignore news that we do not want to hear, sights that are ugly and sounds that are harsh.

And yet, in the West, we still believe in free speech and a free press, even though we know how fragile, unlikely and potentially disruptive such myths are. The same might be said for the myth of free will. High Modernity is often very rough with these myths. How can we reconcile free will with the strands of DNA that can be traced back through the generations to our distant ancestors? How we can make decisions as individuals, when our bodies and minds are structured in this way? How can we defend democracy, if we are drawn to the conclusion that, objectively speaking, such notions as free will, free speech and a free press are, at best, more like mission statements than anything that we are likely to encounter in real life?

The answer partly lies in the pragmatic usefulness of such myths. While it may be impossible to prove that free will exists, it is better to assume that it does than that it does not for practical reasons. Why should we try to improve our lives, if we believe that all our decisions are predestined? The same may be said for other myths. It may be better to believe that humans are rational creatures than that they are not, because otherwise we would not bother to control our passions. It may be better to tell the truth than to lie, although we know that the truth, the whole truth and nothing but the truth is something that only an all-seeing God can provide. It may be better to believe in a free press, even though we know that it is constricted on all sides, because otherwise we would not bother to allow space for public debate. It may be better to believe that there is a benevolent god, rather than a malevolent one or none, because it gives us a greater incentive to be virtuous. And so on.

We believe in such myths not because they are factually true but partly, even perhaps mainly, because they are necessary. We build our towns and villages upon such assumptions. Without them, our lives would even more unreliable than they are. Sometimes, we harden the myths into dogma, to make them sound more official, but we then run into the risk of all-out war with those who do not believe in them or the collapse of the system, if they are shown to be partly wrong. That is the danger of fundamentalism. Under liberalism, we more readily accept the idea that all myths cannot be proved, but that there are better and worse myths. An elector must choose between them, not only at the ballot box, but in his/her conscience.

The entitlement to do so is the driving force behind democratic government. The voter is influenced by his/her direct experience – and indirect as well, by what he/she believes to have happened to others. At the same time, he/she will be governed by the conceptual apparatus brought to the interpretation of these experiences, his/her culture. This includes the bonds of family and class, the memory theatres, rhetoric and the myths that often lie deeply buried in our minds but are sometimes on the surface.

One of the most powerful motives is the intuition that something is *right*, even if it is only expressed by a negative, that something else is wrong. This sense of conviction drives people to vote, and even sometimes into spoiling their ballot papers, and motivates political parties. It also rouses armies, divides nations and sends suicide bombers into supermarkets. Sometimes, there may be clear-cut causes to explain this conviction. We may be driven by a sense of outrage. But more often in the West, it is a mixture of less important causes and the feeling that something is rotten (or not) in the state of Denmark – or wherever – in short, a political *zeitgeist*.

This mood may be deceptive. It may be influenced by perception management or by short-term, feel-good factors, such as a buoyant economy. But having discounted all such factors that may lead to an electoral victory, there remains a mysterious force, the widespread conviction that something is *right* or *wrong* and that a choice has to be made between them. There are many examples, but the Iraq war was a case in point. For those who opposed the war, it often did not matter if it was sanctioned by the Security Council or not. It did not even matter whether the ends justified the means. The invasion was bad in itself. It was not just a matter of opinion.

Sometimes we intuitively assert that we can tell the difference between truth and falsehood, right and wrong, although we may have no logical reason for doing so. Sometimes we are shocked out of our Post-Modern relativities by the sudden thought that *this* is "real", but that *that* is not. The ancient Greeks called it "revelation", others "inspiration". Far from being unusual, it is a common experience. It would be unsettling to live in a world without such an intuition of reality. The philosopher, Immanuel Kant, coined an odd phrase to describe the conviction that sometimes collectively inspires free individuals, who live in societies with a free press, a relatively free voting system and as much freedom of speech as they can handle.

He called it "common sense".

Kant began his academic career as a lecturer in physics at the university in Königsberg, a provincial port on the Baltic, then part of Prussia, but in his late forties, he became a professor in logic and metaphysics. His *Dissertation* in 1770 set out the arguments that he later developed in the *Critique of Judgement* and *Critique of Pure Reason*. He tried to answer the riddle that Descartes had posed, when he made the distinction between objectivity and subjectivity. We may be convinced that something is objectively true, but how can we be sure? We are still slaves of our senses.

Kant concluded that this kind of knowledge was part of our interpretation of our surrounding world. If we say that there are three horses in a field, we have to be able to recognise horses from other animals, in what place they are, and have the skill to count, which are all more complicated mental processes than they may seem. Our knowledge depends partly upon what we can perceive through our senses, but also upon the conceptual apparatus that we bring to that recognition. In both cases, we may be mistaken. Our senses may be deceived and we may mistake cows for horses; but we are still convinced that we know what we know. There are three horses.

Kant anticipated or perhaps influenced the Post-Modernists by pointing out that there was no natural connection between the sign and what it was supposed to signify – or between the concept in our minds and the object in real life. In this way, he distanced himself from those philosophers, who like to believe that the universe was made of numbers or that "God was a watchmaker", and from those who trusted in ideals and absolutes. He was held in disfavour by the later Marxists, social Darwinists and many Freudian psychologists.

But Kant acknowledged that we might passionately believe that something was true and real, even though we might have no logic-proof reason for doing so, and that we might defend that perception with our lives, if necessary. Indeed, we wholly rely in our daily living on the unspoken assumption that some matters are true and others are not, because otherwise there would be no connecting certainty to link a deed with its just reward or one moment with the next. Nor would we be able to talk to our friends or describe a simple phenomenon. It is a necessary myth.

Kant devised five tests for our judgement of reality. If something seems to exist *independently* of our lives, we deem it to be real. It is *universal*, in that we expect everyone to acknowledge that it exists, and *necessary*, in that, by accepting its independence, it is we who have to adjust to its demands. We cannot change them to our own. It may seem to have a purpose, but not a purpose that we can comprehend: we simply assume that it has one. It may accidentally benefit mankind, but this neither adds nor takes away from its reality.

Why, for example, should we believe that some objects are beautiful and others are not? For some philosophers, such as Baumgarten,[4] who pioneered the study of aesthetics, beauty was a matter of sensual pleasure, untouched by the mind. Kant insisted that it was a matter of judgement. If we say that a sunset is beautiful, we do not simply mean that we like it, in the way in which we may like an ice cream. We are stating that it *is* beautiful, whether other people appreciate it or not. Its beauty does not depend upon our likes and dislikes, our needs or desires. It may mean that there will be a thunderstorm. It may give us no benefits whatsoever, other than the pleasure that we derive from seeing it.

Kant borrowed a word from an ancient Roman critic, "Longinus",[5] to describe this kind of beauty, the sublime. Because of its scale or intensity, the sublime lay beyond our understanding. We could not measure what it was. We could not provide it with a function. It was the sign of an external reality beyond our powers of control. It indicated the limits of our understanding, although it would be more accurate to say that *it* did not make us aware of anything. We were aware of *it,* for the sublime was part of our interpretation of the world, an assumption that we were forced to make.

Kant's ideas influenced Coleridge and Wordsworth, and the next generation of Romantic poets, painters and musicians, and how they envisaged their roles as artists and the subjects that they chose for their work. They did not see themselves as social workers or arbiters of fashion, but as "the unacknowledged legislators of mankind", because they were the ones who were most in touch with the reality that lay beyond the circumstances of daily life. "Beauty is truth, truth beauty," wrote Keats in his *Ode to a Grecian Urn*, "that is all/Ye know on earth, and all ye need to know".

The British artist, J.M.W. Turner, who was born in 1775, was an example of this transformation. He studied to become an architectural draftsman, with a keen eye for detail and scale, more of an artist-craftsman than a philosopher. As he grew older, he became less concerned with man-made objects, such as buildings and parks, and more with what only a superhuman force could provide, such as storms at sea and the glow of the setting sun. In Kant's language, Turner's 'determinate' judgement, which meant that he was painting for a particular purpose, such as to satisfy his employer, evolved into a 'reflective' mode, in which he was responding to something which was beautiful in itself, the sublime, a distinction akin to the 'active' and 'passive' moods.

Under the influence of the Romantics, the artist, who painted for a purpose was thought to be a lesser kind of artist than the one who responded to the Sublime and was thus inspired. This led to a confusing double-bluff. Artists, who seemed to be indifferent to wealth and fame, became wealthy and famous, at the expense of those, who painted portraits of families with their dogs and horses in an eighteenth century manner, on commission and for money. And yet even in tackling the most mundane task, it was still possible to be inspired, for the sublime could be found not only in sunsets, but in the tracery of a leaf or the sheen on a thread of hair.

Kant endowed many artists with a high sense of vocation. Their role was to respond intuitively to a reality that was not man-made and had no selfish purpose, and to discover the sublime in simple objects or situations. But soon ready-made imitations of the sublime could be seen everywhere, even in street corner shops, where misty sunrises sold soap. They permeated popular theories as to what was meant by beautiful and it was often hard to tell whether an artist had, like Turner, strapped himself to a mast to paint a storm at sea or merely pretended that he had. Such images quickly degenerated into kitsch, and were used in determinate rather than reflective ways, and so they lost contact with what Kant meant by the sublime.

A golden sunset, featuring a young couple with two children, may seem to be beautiful in itself, sublime even, but when its picture was sold to the Northern Ireland Office, put on the cover of the Belfast Agreement and helped to market the peace process, its beauty was diminished by the way in which it was being used. When objects, which may seem to be beautiful, are drawn into perception management, and artists are used as part of a creative marketing team, they lose their authority. It is no longer their duty to be truthful, but to sell goods or a political dream.

But why should we be interested in something that, according to Kant, we judge to be independent, universal, disinterested and detached from our lives? What is our motive for doing so? It is not faith exactly, for it is riddled with uncertainties, but it could be something that is sometimes mistaken for faith, worship. We are drawn towards the reality that we cannot control, in the effort to find a certainty upon which we can rely. That is, and always has been, the first source of inspiration for the arts.

But in their cultural policies, Modernist governments frequently substitute the determinate judgement for the reflective. It likes to believe that artists paint for a purpose, to satisfy their clients, and can therefore fit into a political agenda. But many artists insist that the discovery of beauty is an end in itself and cannot be separated from the search for reality, which concerns us all. If we suck the arts dry of their original purpose, we may be left with style and political correctness, but not with the quest for truthfulness. From one point of view, they cease to be art.

Gradually, the world becomes a more deceptive place. We start to lose contact with the notion of reality, for our senses can be so easily deceived, and our conceptual apparatus warns us that we may be the victims of fraud, and we start to doubt even the most basic of assumptions, and, imperceptibly, a kind of chaos creeps into our lives.

Inspiration is never blind. It is not a kind of spiritual intoxication. It is more like a recognition that something exists, to which we are intuitively drawn, although we do not know what it is and can only detect a small part of it, a fragment. But we sense that it is there, and want to learn more about it, and to get closer, until we are pulled into its orbit, like a planet around the sun, so that our lives revolve around that tiny sliver of certainty, without which we would spin off into darkness.

Gradually, we adapt and build our lives around that insight, however small it may be, perhaps no more than an acknowledgement that the sun rises and sets, that the seasons change and that spring is not the same as autumn. As we speculate more about these miracles, and wonder about how they could come about, so we are drawn towards developing ways of seeing them more clearly, and from different angles, so that we can become more methodical in our approach. We cannot change reality, but we can alter the conceptual apparatus through which we interpret reality, and learn how to shape our experiences. That is the primary task for the artists and mythmakers, but there is no upwardly moving spiral, which dictates that next year's myths must be better than last year's. We still need common sense.

We start by making unprovable assumptions, which are the only things that we can make, and when they turn out to be wrong or fanciful, we shed them, often slowly and reluctantly, in favour of more illuminating myths. We seek to hand on our refined perceptions to the next generation, until a collection of myths builds into a canon of literature, a religion or an educational system, upon which we think that we can rely. And so, gradually, cultures evolve, based upon an accumulation of insights about reality, which are, at core, unprovable, although we may firmly believe in them.

It is a flexible process: it has to be. The trouble with High Modernity is that it is so unscrupulously attached to its vision of reality that it blocks out all alternatives. It seeks a world that it "can and must control" and when it fails to do so, as it must inevitably fail, it creates a "virtual reality", a *simulacrum*, which better conforms to its assumptions. It stops questioning its myths, at a time when it is trying to impose them upon others, so that even its notions of progress become predictable. Any deviation is interpreted as a mistake or something else that has to be overcome. The juggernaut of High Modernity grinds to a halt, worn down by the obstacles in its way – by the populations to be pacified, the war lords to be defeated, the growing piles of measurement systems, the flies in the ointment and the grit in its wheels.

We do not really need another big mad book to predict what is likely to happen in the Middle East. The writing is on the wall. If the Anglo-American forces fail to impose a form of democracy upon Iraq, then the country will break up into civil war, if it has not done so already. Political pressure from home will demand that the forces should be withdrawn and the result will be seen across the non-Western world as a victory for Islam. Nobody can guess what this may mean, but it is probable that the radicals and fundamentalists in the Islamic world will prosper at the expense of the moderates. If so, the West will face a more formidable enemy than it did even in the depths of the Cold War, which was an Enlightenment schism. Instead, it will be a religious war.

It is a bleak prospect, but what is even more depressing is that, while the West was preparing its plans for the New World Order some twenty years ago, it did not anticipate that something like this might happen. But this was not an isolated mistake. It is a recurring one, for if we remember all the good resolutions that were taken at the Millennium, few have shown many signs of progress and some are going backwards. For a civilization that has come to depend a great deal upon predictive models, our skill at guessing what may happen next seems to be very limited.

'Virtual reality' is the world as we would like it to be. It may look similar to the real world. It may have the same beaches and the same sky, but it is a world that *we can and must control*. It is a place where friendships are made in Chat Rooms, where a six-foot-tall, thirty-five-year-old company director, who likes swimming and jazz, meets a twenty-five-year-old blonde designer, who is into dancing and foreign travel. It is also the world of the global management consultants and those who believe that by using the tactics of 'shock and awe', democracy can be imposed on the Middle East.

When political leaders become careless about the sources of their authority in a democracy, they are more likely to fake the results. They devise new targets and measurement systems, whose purpose is not to find out what is happening, but to win the next election. An accumulation of such facts and figures leads to an impression of a society that is within their control. Any signs to the contrary are buried, which is the task of the perception manager. Maintaining an illusion of political success is how some ministers of culture earn their places at the top tables of government.

A virtual democracy, which has embraced High Modernity as its state religion, is an enclosed system of self-fulfilling prophecies. It is convincing, practical and, for those who are ready to accept its rules and restrictions, reassuring. It can be comfortable, affluent and charming. It is not without a conscience. It is always making good resolutions. It really enjoys doing so. It can raise vast amounts of money for this good cause or that. But when it comes face to face with a difficult decision, one that may (like global warming) change its life styles or (like terrorism) upset its sense of security, it shows the signs of panic. It hides its head under the bedclothes or seizes a machine gun to fire in all directions. It has no common sense. It is always a bit out of touch with the rest of the world. As a result, it misses the point, habitually and compulsively, and all its good resolutions are forgotten by 1 February.

It as if we are sitting at a feast and our host has locked the doors against all intruders, but at the back of our minds, we still know that they are there. And so we eat to remind ourselves that we are the lucky ones, and we eat to reassure ourselves that we deserve our good fortune, and we eat humbly, having said grace, in honour of our ancestors who made sacrifices on our behalf, but while we eat, we secretly expect a knock at the door, a very loud knock, one that is hard to ignore. Who will answer it? Should anyone do so? We draw lots, democratic to the last, until, finally, an unlucky messenger is forced to accept the short straw.

He/she goes to the doors, slowly opens them, and quickly closes them again, but, in that brief moment, light floods in, an intolerable light, one that reveals the debris of our lives, but light nonetheless, and beyond the doors, we can glimpse the outside world. We do not want to see too much of it. Enough is enough, but what we experience then may transform our lives. The ancient Greeks called it revelation, for it is not speculative, and it is not virtual reality, and we cannot forget it. We build our languages, myths, arts and sciences around these nanoseconds of certainty that accumulate over time and start to form what we recognise as our cultures.

But sometimes we do not want to open the doors at all. It is too risky. We sit around the tables in the allocated places that we know too well, until darkness and the sound of the knocking deadens our senses and stifles our souls. With each moment that passes, it becomes more difficult for us to move. We become inert, hard-faced and settled in our ways. We control our little world. Nothing can shift us. We do not have to climb aboard the juggernaut of High Modernity. We are that juggernaut.

Notes

1. Although this example pre-dated New Labour and OFCOM, Thames Television, a highly successful company, was widely thought to have lost its license, because it enraged Mrs. Thatcher's government by screening *Death on the Rock*, a documentary reconstruction of the killing of three IRA suspects in Gibraltar.
2. "Bloggers" are "web loggers".
3. Reporters Without Borders has established a ranking system of countries in terms of their freedom of the press. The top countries in 2003/4 were Finland, Iceland, Holland, Norway, Ireland, Denmark, Slovakia and Switzerland. The lowest ranking country was North Korea, followed by Burma, China (mainland), Turkmenistan, Eritrea, Vietnam, Nepal, Saudi Arabia and Iran.
4. Alexander Gottlieb Baumgarten (1714-1762)
5. "Longinus" was a false name – and I do not know the real one.
6. John Keats: *Ode on a Grecian Urn*

Index

Abramov, Fyodor, 68
Adams, Gerry, 78-80, 86-87
Aeschylus, 104, 109
Afghanistan, 16
Agamemnon, 105
Aherne, Bertie (Taoiseach of the
    Republic of Ireland), 84
Al-Matashi, Ibrahim, 122
Al-Qaeda, 16
Ambassadors, The, 72
American Bar Association, 109
Anglo-Irish Agreement, 77
Anschutz Entertainment Group, 31
Apollo, 65, 105
Areopagitica, 151
Aristotle, 115-116
Arnold, Matthew, 129-130, 143
Art of Memory, The, 133
Arts Council of Great Britain, 13, 60-62
Arts Councils (in Great Britain), 131
A Short Organum, 116
Assembly (Northern Ireland), 77, 84-85
At The Edge of the Union, 108-111
Athens, 103-104
Atreus, House of, 104
Auschwitz, 47, 48

Baghdad, 87, 89, 91, 151
Bangalore, 21
Bali (bombing), 16
Bankside Power Station, 144-145
Battersea Power Station, 144
Barbican Centre (London), 10, 127
Barry, Charles, 143
Battle of the Boyne, 79
Baudrillard, Jean, 46, 55, 59, 93, 101
Bauhaus Movement, 135, 144
Baumgarten, Alexander Gottlieb, 155, 161
Bayley, Stephen, 28-29, 33
BBC Experience, The, 121

Bedouin (tribes), 7-9, (chief) 9-17
Beecham, Sir Thomas, 143
Beer-sheba, 12
Beijing, 92
Belfast, 13, 127, 148
Belfast Agreement, The, 75, 77, 81-84,
    87, 157
Belfast Telegraph, 88
Berlin, 22, 26-27
Berlusconi, Silvio, 95
Bertelsmann, 91, 100
Big Brother, 97
Birmingham, 21
Birt, Sir John, 75, 112, 120, 125
Bishop, Patrick, 112
Bishop, W.D., 101, 116
Blair, Tony, 17, 18, 32, 43-45, 62, 82-86,
    89-90, 96, 97, 112, 122, 124, 140,
    147-148
Blair, Cherie, 32, 147
Blair Revolution, The, 23, 95
Blair's Wars, 88, 126
Bloody Sunday, 79
Bloody Friday, 79
Bobbitt, Philip, 23, 32, 43
Boots the Chemists, 30
Bosnia, 76
Boston Globe, 89
Bourn, Sir John, 31
Bouvet, Joachim, 38
Breakfast News (BBC), 90
Brecht, Bertolt, 116
British Broadcasting Company, 114
British Broadcasting Corporation (BBC),
    12-14, 28, 63, 75, 82, 89-90, 93,
    96-100, 102, 108-111, 114-129, 131,
    139-141
British-Irish Forum, 77
British Library, 127
British National Party, 85

British Telecom (BT), 116, 139
Brittan, Leon (as Home Secretary), 109-111
Brixton (riots), 13
Broadcasting House (BBC), 121
Broadcasting in the 1990s, 117, 125
Brothers and Sisters, 68-71
Bucharest, 27
Buckingham Palace, 146
Bugsby Moor, 28
Bush, George W., 17, 22, 44, 84, 87

Cable by Choice, 101, 116, 125
Caff, J.T., 60, 72
Cairo, 87
Campbell, Alastair, 44, 90, 122-124
Campbell, Gregory, 108, 109, 111
Canary Wharf, 77
Cardiff, 127
Cartesianism, 36, 38-39
Castor, 132
Ceos, 132
Chadwick, Paul, 100
Changing Rooms, 45
Channel 4, 28, 123
Chaplin, Charles, 21
Charing Cross, 146
Charities, 130
Chechnya, 76
Checkland, Sir Michael, 109, 112
Chernenko, Konstantin, 68, 71
Chernobyll, 92
Chomsky, Noam, 21
Choneweth, Neil, 100
Churchill, Sir Winston, 114-115
Cicero, Marcus Tullius, 106-107, 112, 132
City of London, 29
City Hall, London, 145
Civil Rights Marches (Northern Ireland), 134
Clark, Steve, 125
Clash of Civilizations, The, 22, 32, 88
Cleverdon, Douglas, 118
Clinton, President William J., 21, 23, 44, 75, 78, 87
Clytemnestra, 105
CNN, 91
Cold War Theatre, 72
Coleridge, Samuel Taylor, 156
Collapse of the American Management Mystique, The, 122, 125

Comédie Française, 129
Conran, Terence, 147
Contemporary Review, 72, 125
Conservative Party, 11, 28, 51-52, 140
Copernicus, 35
County Hall, London, 145
Craig, Sir James, 79
Creative Britain, 64
Critique of Judgement, 154
Critique of Pure Reason, 154
Croatia, 24, 26
Culture and Consensus, 62-63, 72
Culture, Media and Sport, Department of (DCMS), 7, 63, 131

Dadaism, 41
Daily Telegraph, 58
Dali, Salvador, 145
Darwin, Charles, 39, 135
Da Vinci, Leonardo, 65-66
Death on the Rock, 161
Declaration of Support (see *Belfast Agreement*)
De Inventione, 106
De Montfort, Simon, 143
Della Pittura, 65-66
Democrats, 75
Democratic Unionist Party (DUP), 78, 85-86, 108
De Saussure, Ferdinand, 41
Descartes, René, 35-36, 154
De Valera, Eamonn, 79-80
Dialogues, 104
Diana, Princess of Wales, 63
Disney Corporation, 91, 93, 100
Disneyland, 28
Dissertation (Kant), 154
Dodin, Lev, 68, 70-72, 128, 130-131,138
Dome, The Millennium, 20-21, 24, 28, 30-35, 62, 121, 138, 145
Downing Street Years, 113
Drumcree, 93
Dr. Zhivago, 69
Dubner, Stephen J., 58
Dunford, John, 52
Dyke, Greg, 122-123

Easter Rising, 79, 81
Eco, Umberto, 38, 46
Education and Skills, Department of, 51-52
Education, Sciences and the Arts, 60

Edward the Confessor, 143
Einstein, Albert, 41
Eire (see Ireland, Republic of)
Elgar, Sir Edward, 63
Eliot, T.S., 36, 46
Elizabeth II, 32
End of History, The, 22
Enlightenment, The, 36-39, 41, 81
Entertainments Tax, 129
Esslin, Martin, 125
European Community, 27
European Convention on Human Rights, 148
European Union (EU), 23-24, 27, 85, 86
Excalibur, 44
L'Explication de l'Arithmétique Binaire, 38

False Dawn, 55, 59
Faith Zone, 30, 34
Families Against Intimidation and Terror (FAIT), 88
Famine of 1847, 79
Fay, Marie-Thérèse, 88
Fender, Brian, 52
Féile au Phoail, 79
Festival of Britain, 29
Fianna Fáil, 80
Financial Times, 110
Firdos Square, 89
First Amendment (to the US Constitution), 150
Fox, 89, 96, 151
Foreign Affairs Select Committee, 122
Formalism, 135
Foster, Norman, 138, 145
Frazer, Sir James, 40
Freakeconomics, 58
Freedoms (of the Press, Speech and Worship), 150-151
Freud, Sigmund, 41, 155
Frost Programme, The, 120
Fu His, 38
Fukuyama, Francis, 22, 55
Furies, The, 105
Fuzzy Monsters, 125

Galileo, 35
General Electric, 100
Geneva Convention, 16
Gherkin, The, 145
Giddens, Anthony, 18, 23, 25, 32-33, 38, 40, 92

Gilligan, Andrew, 123
Gladstone, W.E., 80
Glasgow, 127
Golden Bough, The, 40
Golden Globe (St. Paul's Cathedral), 144, 146
Good Friday Agreement (see Belfast Agreement)
Gorbachev, Mikhail, 40, 68-70
Gorgias, 103, 112
Gorki, Maxim, 70
Gould, Philip, 44
Grade, Michael, 28-29
Granada Television, 120
Grand Projêts de M. Mitterand, 127
Gray, John, 55-56, 59
Gray's Anatomy, 36
Great Dictator, The, 21
Great Exhibition of 1851, 28
Green Party, 60
Greenwich, 144
Greenwich Observatory, 20
Gropius, Walter, 135-136
Guantanamo Bay, 16
Gulbenkian Foundation, 60
Gulf Oil, 118-119
Gulf War, 89, 91
Gulf War Did Not Take Place, The, 93, 101
Gutenberg Galaxy, The, 100

Habitat, 147
Hampstead, 144
Hare, David, 69
Harris, Robert, 112
Harvey, Robert, 23, 32
Heaney, Seamus, 79, 88
Herder, J. G., 81
Hewison, Robert, 60, 62-64, 72
Higher Education Funding Council, 52
Hinduja Family Foundation, 30
Hippocratic Oath, 36
Hirst, Damien, 142, 146
Hitler, Adolf, 17, 62
Holbein Hans, the Younger, 66, 72
Holland, Tony, 54, 58
Hollywood, 83, 148
Home Rule, 80
Hong Kong, 137-138
Horrie, Chris, 125
Hosenball, Mark, 108

House of Commons, 107, 123
Houses of Parliament, 143
Hugo, Victor, 129
Hume, John, 78, 83
Husák, Gustav, 92
Huntington, Samuel P., 22, 32, 88
Hussey, Marmaduke, 110, 112
Huxley, Thomas, 39, 41

I Ching, 38
Imperium, 112
Implementation Review Unit (IRU), 52
Independent, The, 84, 88, 149
India, Government of, 17
Ingham, Bernard, 100
Ingrams, Adam, 88
Independent Television (ITV), 28
Information and Security Conference
   (Colorado Springs), 89
Inside Story, 122
International Association of Theatre
   Critics (IATC), 10, 19, 26, 68
International Monetary Fund, 56
Inuit, 11
Iraq, 16, 99, 148, 151, 154, 159
Ireland, Republic of, 25, 79, 80
Irish Constitution, 79
Irish Republican Army (IRA), 13, 76-78,
   84-87, 109, 110, 134
Israel, State of, 7, 15
Israel, Friends of, 10, 14

Jarry, Alfred, 41
Jay, Peter, 120
John, King of England, 143
Jones, Nicholas, 100, 126
Journey Without End, 138

Kabul, 16
Kampfner, John, 88, 124, 126
Kandinsky, Wassily, 135
Kant, Immanuel, 131, 154-7
Keats, John, 156, 161
Kelly, Dr. David, 123
Kelly, Tom, 82, 91
Keneally, Thomas, 134
Kennan, George, 22
Kepler, Johann, 35
King Lear, 119
King Oedipus, 98
Kissinger, Henry, 32
Klee, Paul, 135

Knesset, 12
Königsberg, 154
Kosovo, 16, 89

Labour Party (see also New Labour), 17,
   140, 144
Laden, Osama bin, 148
Laity, Mark, 89, 91
Lasdun, Sir Denys, 143
La Ville Radieuse, 135-136
Learning and Skills Council (LSC), 51
Learning Zone, 30
Leader, The, 80, 88
Le Corbusier, 135-136
Leibnitz, Gottfried Wilhelm, 36, 38
Lenin, Vladimir Ilych, 54
Leningrad (see also St. Petersburg), 27,
   68-69
LenSoviet Theatre for the Education of
   the Young, 27
Levitt, Steven, 49-51
Liberal Democratic Party, 60
Liberal Party of Great Britain, 10-11, 14,
   28, 60, 131
Liberal Party's Arts and Broadcasting
   Committee, 10
Liddle, Roger, 23, 95
Liverpool, 127
Local Government Act, 53
Locke, John, 36, 151
Locke, Robert R., 119, 122, 125
London, 16, 17, 137, 142-147
London Eye, 142, 146
London School of Economics (LSE), 55
London Weekend Television (LWT), 112-
   113, 120
'Longinus', 156
Lyotard, Jean-François, 43, 46, 86
Lyubimov, Yuri, 69

Maastricht Treaty, 27
McCann Erikson, 82
McCartney, Jenny, 88
McChesney, Robert, 91, 93, 97, 100
McGuinness, Martin, 82, 108-111
McKinsey & Co. (management
   consultants), 117
McLuhan, Marshall, 91
Madrid, 16
Madurai, 21
Maggie's Militant Tendency, 120
Major, John, MP, 61, 78-79

Making Peace, 74, 75
Mallie, Eamonn, 112
Maly Drama Theatre, 68, 70-71, 130
Managing Britannia, 52
Mandelson, Peter, 23, 28, 95
Mao Tse Tung, 92, 112
Marks & Spencer, 29
Marks, Karl, 54
Marxism, 155
Meacher, Michael, MP, 45
Media Mates, 100
Memory Theatre, 64, 132-135
Michelangelo, Buonarroti, 66
Microsoft, 24, 25, 139-142, 149
Mitchell, George, 74, 75, 77-80, 83, 87-89, 100
Mill, John Stuart, 151
Millennium Dome (see Dome)
Milne, Alasdair, 109, 110, 112
Milton, John, 150, 151
Mirror, The, 44-45
Modernity, history of, 34-46
Money Zone, 29
Moran, D.P., 80-81
Morrissey, Mike, 88
Morris, Estelle (Baroness Morris of Yardley), 52
Mowlam, Mo, MP, 83
Murdoch, Rupert, 89, 91, 95-96, 109-110, 117
Murdoch Archipelago, The, 100-101, 112
Murgiyanto, Sal, 19
Myth and Modernity, 35

Nablus, 87
National Audit Office, 31
National Arts and Media Strategy, 62
National Campaign for the Arts, 60
National Foundation for the Arts and Sciences, 61
National Gallery, 143
National Heritage, Department of, 11
National Interest, The, 22
National Lottery, 28-29, 61, 145
NATO, 16, 89
National Socialist Party, 17
National Theatre, (Royal National Theatre), 143
Negev Desert, 7-15, 87
Neo-Cons, 21, 55
New Approach Towards Investment in Culture, 63

Newcastle, 127
New Delhi, 25
New Labour, 7, 17, 20, 23-24, 28-29, 52-53, 63, 139-141, 161
New Millennium Experience, 24, 28-30, 32
Newscorp, 91, 100, 109
News International, 109
Newsweek, 138
Newton, Sir Isaac, 36
'New World Order', 21, 36, 159
New York, 16, 137, 147
Nicholson, Adam, 20, 31-32
Nobel Peace Prize, 83
NORAID, 74, 87
Northern Ireland, 14, 25, 74-89, 157

Ode to a Grecian Urn, 151, 161
OFCOM (Office of Communications), 51
OFSTED (Office of Standards in Education), 51
Olympic Games (2012), 32
Omagh, 83
Orestes, 105
Oresteia, The, 104-105
Organisation for Economic Co-operation and Development, 56
Orwell, George, 151
L'Osservatore Romano, 76
O'Sullivan, John, 84
O'Toole, Fintan, 82

Page, Bruce, 91, 100-101, 112
Paisley, Dr. Ian, 78-80, 86
Palace of Westminster, 143, 145
Panorama, 93, 120
Paramount Pictures, 118-119
Paris, 93, 127
Pasternak, Boris, 69
Peace Process (in Northern Ireland), 74-87
Pekashino, 68, 70
Performances Tables, 53
Petersburg (see also Leningrad), 27, 68
Philosophy of Irish Ireland, The, 80
Pick, John, 52-53, 58
Plato, 34-35, 46, 67, 103-104, 150
Platonism, 13
Poetics, The, 115
Poetry of the Celtic Races, The, 88
Poland, 26

Police Service of Northern Ireland, 84-85
Policy Studies Institute, 60
Pollux, 132
Porter, Roy, 38, 46
Post-Modernity, 42-43
Powell, Colin, 123
Prague, 92
Pravda, 69
PriceWaterhouseCooper (PWC), 146
Principles of Mathematics, The, 41
Private Eye, 125
Programme Development Group (BBC), 121
Protherough, Robert, 52-53, 58
Provisional IRA, 109
Provisional IRA, The, 112
Public Service Broadcasting (PSB), 111, 115, 120
Public Service Principle, 130
Pythagoras, 35-36, 67

Qualifications and Curriculum Auithority (QCA), 51
Queen's University, Belfast, 80
Question Time, 96

Rampton, S., 100
Reagan, Ronald, 96, 109
Real Lives, 108
Reichstag, 17
Reith, John (Lord Reith), 110, 114-116, 124
Renan, Ernst, 88
Rendon, John W., 89, 93
Reporters without Borders, 161
Republic, The, 34
Return of the Strong, The, 23
Reuters, 89
Richard Rogers Partnership, 28
Richards, Steve, 88
Richmond, 144
Romantic Movement, 81, 156
Royal Court Theatre, 69, 70
Royal Festival Hall, 143
Royal Shakespeare Company, 144
Royal Ulster Constabulary (RUC), 76, 85, 110
Russell, Bertrand, 41
Russia, 16, 67-72
Russian Orthodox Church, 27

Saatchi, Charles, 145
Saddam Hossein, 16, 89, 93, 122

St. Catherine's College, Oxford, 120
St. Mary's College, Liverpool, 120
St. Paul's Cathedral, 144, 146
St. Petersburg, 68
Salford, 127
Sampson, Clare, 30
Scarborough, Milton, 35, 46
Schiller, Friedrich, 129
Schindler's Ark, 134
Scopas, 132
Scott, Giles Gilbert, 144
Seagram, 100
Self Portrait zone, 29
Semonides, 64, 132
Shakespeare, William, 38, 66, 72, 129
Shaw, George Bernard, 138
Singapore, 137
Sinn Féin, 77-79, 82, 84-86, 93, 108
Sixsmith, Martin, 91
Sky television, 89
Smith, Chris, MP, 44-45, 63, 72
Smith, Sydney R.J., 143
Smyth, Marie, 88
Solzhenitsyn, Alexander, 69
Social Democratic and Labour Party (SDLP), 78, 85
Social Role of Theatre Critic, The, 67
Socialist Workers Party, 85
Socrates, 35, 103-105
Solidarity, 27
Somme, Battle of, 79
Sony, 100
Soros, George, 58, 59
South Africa, 76
South Armagh, 85, 93
Soviet Union, 16, 22, 27, 40, 54, 62, 67-68, 107, 135, 152
Spice Girls, The, 63
Springer, Jerry, 97
Standards Board of England, 53-54
Stalin, 54, 62, 69
Stanislavsky, Konstantin, 70
Stauber, J., 100
Stormont, 78. 82, 84
Stuff Happens, 69
Sullivan, Louis, 135
Sultans of Spin, 100, 126
Sunday Telegraph, 88
Sunday Times, 108-109
Sunningdale Agreement, 77
Surrealism, 41

Sydney, 137
Sydney, Sir Philip, 66
Szajna, Josef, 48

Taganka Theatre, 69-70
Taliban, 16
Tate Britain, 142, 143
Tate, Henry, 143, 145
Tate Liverpool, 145
Tate Modern, 142, 144-145
Tate, St. Ives, 145
TCI, 100
Tesco, 30
Thames Television, 161
Thatcher, Margaret H. (Baroness Thatcher
    of Kesteven), 13, 61, 87, 96, 102, 108-
    113, 115-116, 121, 123, 126, 161
Theaetetus, 103-104, 112
Theatre of the Absurd, 41
Theory of Relativity, 41
Third Way, The, 23
Thomas, Dylan, 118
Tienanmen Square, 21, 92
Timaeus, 35
Time-Warner, 91, 93, 96, 100
Times, The, 52, 58, 96, 120
Timon of Athens, 72
Tito, Marshal, 27
Today programme, 123
Tolstoy, Leo, 69-70
Toxteth (riots), 13
Trimble, David (Lord Trimble of
    Lisnagarvey), 62, 82-84, 86
Trojan War, 104
Truman, President Harry, 22
Turner, J.M.W., 156-157
Twelfth Night, 128
TW3 (*That Was The Week That Was*), 115

Ukraine, 16
Ulster Freedom Fighters (UFF), 78
Ulster Unionists, 82, 84, 85
Uncle Vanya, 73, 98
Under Milk Wood, 118
United Nations (UN), 23

United States of America (USA), 15, 24-25
UNESCO, 10, 26
UN Security Council, 16, 23, 123-124,
    147
Universal Declaration of Human Rights,
    150

Vatican, 76
Veljanovski, C.G., 101, 116
Viacom, 100
Viewers and Listeners Association, 121
Virtual Murdoch, 100
Voice of America, 116
Voltaire, 151

Wages of Spin, 100
Walden, George, 125
Waterloo Station, 142, 146
Waugh, Evelyn, 123
Weapons of Mass Deception, 100
Weekend World, 120
West Belfast Community Arts Festival,
    75
West End (London), 129
West Kowloon Cultural Development,
    138
Westminster Abbey, 143
Wilson, Harold (Baron Wilson of
    Rievaulx), 144
Windows (Microsoft), 139, 141
'Witkacy' (Stanisław Ignacy), 41
Wolfowitz, Paul, 22
Wordsworth, William, 156
World Services (BBC), 116
World Trade Organisation, 56
World War I, 149
Wren, Sir Christopher, 144
Wyatt, Woodrow, 110

Yates, Francis, 132
Yeats, W.B, 64, 81
Young, Stuart, 110
Yugoslavia, 24, 26, 27

Zagreb, 24, 26
Zeus, 132

Printed in the United Kingdom
by Lightning Source UK Ltd.
122060UK00001B/154-366/A